Mining For My Voice

How A Meek And Scared Boy Uncovered A
World-Rattling Voice

Ryan D. Hall

Edited And Published By Royal Hearts Media

Foreword By Lisa Pachence, Master Certified Coach

This book is a memoir. It reflects the author's present recollections of experiences over time. Some names and characteristics have been changed, some events have been compressed, and some dialogue has been recreated.

All photos from the author's personal collection.

For speaking and interview opportunities please email royalheartscoaching@gmail.com

ISBN (Paperback) 9798791909404
ISBN (Hardcover) 9798358928145

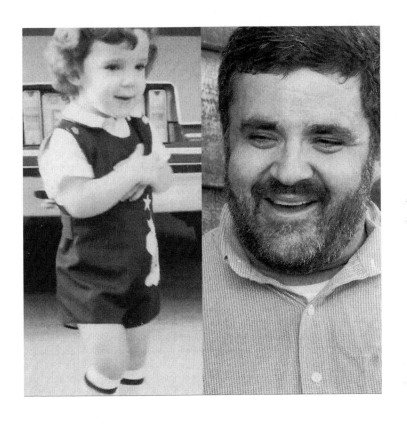

Table Of Contents:

Dedication

To my inner child.

You always wanted to speak.

You always wanted to share yourself and your story.

You always wanted to share your voice.

Thank you for letting me share your story and your voice for you.

Our voice and *our* story.

Foreword

By Lisa Pachence,
Master Certified Coach, Author, Speaker,
Founder of LP Coaching

SELF-AWARENESS (A Healing Revolution)

As a Master Certified Coach, a personal development nerd, a business owner, a woman, as well as a new mother, I've personally and professionally witnessed this phenomenon: more women than men take on work in personal/self development. Our biology leans naturally towards nurturing, inner reflection, and community. Not to mention that our society more easily accepts women seeking, embracing, and speaking about personal development.

For a man to be leading from the inside out - healing generational trauma and walking that path of self-awareness, self-healing, and self-actualization and modeling it for his world – that changes things.

Ryan's choice to tread this path of heartbreak and heart-make is an act of courage that we can and should take a page from.

Not just because it's my opinion, but because scientific studies repeatedly show that we cannot generate sustainable joy, fulfillment, and healthy relationships without doing our own inner work (EQi-2.0)

Personal healing and self-awareness is the basis for having emotional intelligence. And high emotional intelligence is our single greatest predictive factor of success and happiness. Further, it's scientifically proven to improve one's ability to lead teams, create meaningful relationships, and generate effective change. (EQi-2.0)

Socially and culturally, we're headed towards a revolution in our priorities. No longer will we tolerate the 9-5, a paycheck with benefits, the title, the status, the vacation home, the travel, and the status quo of "just how it is." External trophies no longer carry the same weight.

What now carries weight is the ability to find and create joy and purpose in our lives. In other words, growing our emotional intelligence.

Many now seek this self-actualization through their careers, which is what the Great Resignation (2021-2022) is truly about. We no longer tolerate the finite games of profit and corporate power. We'd rather look toward the infinite games of legacy, passion, mission, and fulfillment based on our hearts calling, which

Simon Sinek highlights in his book *The Infinite Game.*

And that is what I see this book being about: an everyday man's mission to leave a legacy and to find fulfillment in his zone of joy and genius.

I don't know about you, but that's a revolution I'd gladly buy into!

The thing about this revolution is that there's no VIP ticket to get you in the door. It's a commitment to actively, consistently, and persistently engaging with deep, soul-level meaning for a lifetime.

This revolution isn't about sitting in the stands and judging or analyzing. Just like you can't pay someone to get fit and form rock-hard abs without doing the challenging work, you can't be a passive participant in your personal transformation. You must do the reps yourself, with the understanding that accountability and help is often a prerequisite to sustaining a path of transformation.

This revolution is about people like Ryan choosing to do the hard stuff every day to serve a legacy that lives long beyond our next paycheck. It's about understanding and forgiving our past. It's about listening for the love and lessons instead of the blame and shame. It's about bettering our character, our community, and our future selves. And it's about filling our own bucket with goodness, kindness, and compassion so that we can make an impact through our embodied values. This way, we can change the systemic traumas that have been handed down through generations.

And the most delicious part of this revolution is this: the roots we grow through nurturing our agency, purpose, and impact have limitless ways of changing generations to come.

Because the best way to change other people's behavior is by modeling and embodying that behavior ourselves, walking the decades-long path of healing and self-discovery, and bravely expressing it as an invitation for others to join the journey.

That is what emotional intelligence, personal transformation and personal development can do for the world. That's modern-day, soul-first leadership.

And THAT is making a difference.

SELF-EXPRESSION
(A Revolution In Voice and Vulnerability)

While self-awareness is the root of all healing, self-expression is the trunk and branches of a happy, successful life. It's the visible representation of the inner landscape.

The authentic form of self-expression and voice is not just about saying something, but living it. It's about having so much conviction in your message that you're willing to stand in front of your world - either live or virtually - and speak about something uncomfortable and deeply vulnerable. And while this may feel unreasonable, you feel a soul obligation to share your message.

One cannot do this and sustain it without the foundation of self-awareness and healing. Otherwise, it's just another nice-sounding catchphrase that at best, may get liked by a few bystanders and forgotten. Like Brene Brown says, "just another catchy cat poster in my office."

Voice isn't about saying something to achieve an outcome or make a buck. It's saying something on behalf of your values, without knowing or attaching yourself to the outcome.

Your message may make people uncomfortable. It may make you uncomfortable to deliver your message, yet, once again, you feel a soul-level obligation to push past the discomfort to deliver that message. When you do the work to be powerfully self-expressed, that is voice at its highest level of impact.

Voice is an interesting cultural concept. Phrases like "having a voice", "finding your voice", and "raising your voice" are common. We treat it like a thing or a tool, when really it's a way of being and something to embody.

We're often taught as children to be seen and not heard. Go play quietly, be small, make things more comfortable for others. Even if our parents don't maliciously impart this, we're socially conditioned that way.

Just look at how crying children on commercial airline flights are treated! We end up placing so many constraints on what we should say, when we should say it, how we should say it, that we end up NEVER saying it and losing our ability to turn up the volume on what's meaningful to us.

Nobody's voice is ever lost, though our past may cause us to turn the volume way down. Voice is always there, waiting and hibernating until we're ready to experience the revolution of tuning into and amplifying our message.

Only after we've forgiven our past and given ourselves permission to be whole and complete in the present, can we take the step to tune our internal radio station to the right frequency and blast that sucker when it's time. This creates ripple effects as we develop a kind connection to our intuition and to where our internal compass needle (or radio dial) is pointing.

Voice is not inherently safe, convenient, or comfortable. Voice is vulnerability, especially when it comes from the selfless desire to better ourselves and others. To me, that's the definition of being a thought leader - leading with voice and vulnerability.

And there is nothing so enrolling and inspiring than a person who uses their voice and vulnerability to support others to use their own voice.

As you read this book, I hope it ignites your passion to develop self-awareness and self-expression as a means to revolutionize happiness and a greater purpose. I hope Ryan's book fans the flames of your courage so you can turn up the volume of your voice and vulnerability, as a way of healing forward. Then, pass it along.

Cheers to the revolution of self-awareness and self-expression, and the path towards healing ourselves and our society. Onward!

Introduction

"No matter what anybody tells you, words and ideas can change the world." - John Keating (Robin Williams) *Dead Poets Society*.

February 10, 2022

I'm coming to you from a laundromat in Stamford, CT. This is a standard Thursday night after work.

Earlier as I was loading my laundry, I managed to drop a brand new bottle of detergent on the ground, spilling half of it. I sheepishly got the attendant at the laundromat to help me clean it up and I ended up with barely enough to wash my clothes. This is an ordinary Thursday night after work.

Yet 48 hours ago, I did something that my younger self would have thought unconscionable and far from ordinary.

Two days ago, I delivered a virtual talk. A talk, the preparation of which has inspired in no small part, this book. A talk that was all about taking a shovel, and in some cases a pickaxe and dynamite, and mining for the world-rattling voice that lay dormant inside me for most of my life. A talk that I pray encouraged the audience to strike gold with their own world-rattling voices.

As a child, for all intents and purposes, I was silent for years. I was terrified to share who I was and terrified to share my story. I would spend upwards of 22 hours a day in my room with the door closed playing video games and watching TV. To say that I've come a long way from that kid to the man who takes pride and joy in sharing his voice and message with the world is an understatement of the big and honkin' variety.

I remember when I first shared with my editor that I wanted to write a memoir, she was all over the idea. However, I thought I was filled with delusions of grandeur.

Famous celebrities write memoirs about their lives.

The last time I checked, I'm neither famous nor a celebrity.

I mean, I read Gregg Allman's memoir A *Cross To Bear* multiple times as I was researching and writing *Hello Again.* I drew inspiration from much of the character of Jimmy Holliday from Gregg's life. Granted, the vast majority of Jimmy's character was based on my Dad, but a good deal of it was based on the Midnight Rider himself.

Brother Gregory's book is a powerfully written memoir about a complicated man. Gregg's story starts after his father was murdered when he was two years old. And it follows Gregg's rise, fall, and rise again in the music business. In his book, he shares how he wrote one of the Allman Brothers' most famous songs on an ironing board cover with the soot from a burned-out match. Gregg's musical journey started by being a vocalist purely out of necessity to becoming one of rock's most endearing and enduring voices. And his story involves plenty of sex, drugs, and rock and roll.

Sex, drugs, and rock and roll - three things my story does not have.

One of the most influential books I've ever read in any context is by a retired Navy SEAL turned ultramarathoner and motivational speaker, David Goggins. His memoir/self-help manifesto is *Can't Hurt Me: Master Your Mind And Defy The Odds*. In that book, David shares how he fought off health issues, family trauma, and unfortunate injuries during his SEAL training to go through three different hell weeks during three different SEAL training classes as he became a SEAL. Navy SEAL training is infamous for being the most stringent and challenging training of all American special forces. Yet Goggins did it three different times.

Goggins' story has racism, learning difficulties, and hints of organized crime. Except for my learning difficulties, my story has none of that.

I'm an author, podcaster, book publisher, and life coach. My story may be seen by many as ordinary. However, the voice I have mined for and cultivated over the years is anything but. And I pray this book helps you to find your own voice so that you can rattle your world with your message.

**

What you're going to find in this book are stories about important events and people in my life. Many of these events and people taught me at the time that my voice didn't matter. These events may have led me to believe that what I had to say was insignificant.

That I was insignificant.

Many of the events I'm going to share illustrate how I changed who I am and what I'm about to make others feel more comfortable around me. And not in the warm, comfy fireplace, transformative way. But in the "you've got to play the game, Ryan" sort of way.

However many of the stories I share are about people, places, and creatures who have taught me that what I have to say matters. That my voice matters.

Long story short, this book is about my personal transformation. And if this book helps one person begin to create their own personal transformation to uncover their voice, then I've done my job.

So gather 'round, drop the needle on your favorite record, take your shoes off and get comfortable. It's story time with Uncle Ryan.

This is my story of how a meek and terrified boy grew into a man who uncovered a world-rattling voice.

Chapter 1

My story begins on a dark and stormy mid-March Saturday in 1977. Tuscaloosa, Alabama was under a tornado warning right as the cord was cut. I guess you could say that I was that non-metaphorical storm cloud.

I was a large baby - a chunky 10 pounds and 4 ounces. Not only was I late entering this world - my original due date was at the end of February - I came out of the oven with breathing problems. My parents have told me that it took doctors a good eight minutes before they could get me to cry.

One of my favorite pictures I've ever seen is right as the doctor hands baby Ryan to Mom for the first time after the cord was cut. Mom is exhausted after she had to have an emergency C-section. Dad is beaming. And I'm crimson red.

"They call Alabama the Crimson Tide..." am I right?

This memory may have even been from the very day I was born. I was laying in my mother's arms as my eyes slowly opened to the world. I remember the walls in the room being this sort of mustard yellow, and my entire family was there. They were just looking at me.

It's as if everybody was saying to me 'Hi Ryan, welcome to the world. Now start talking.'

For the first couple of years after I was born, my family lived in this small rental house in Midtown Tuscaloosa. I don't remember the house nor do I remember where it was located. But I have heard stories.

And as Mom was pregnant with my sister Ivy, they knew they needed an upgrade. So they bought and moved into a three-bedroom, ranch-style house on Tuscaloosa's east side right off Hargrove Road. This was where I actually grew up.

And in this house was this sofa set - a sofa with a matching chair and ottoman. With the understanding that this sofa set was probably purchased in 1979, furniture fashion was quite different. So I'm willing to give Mom and Dad a pass on this.

This sofa set was on a different planet of ugly. It had this ornate pattern accented with various shades of brown and orange. On the arms of both the sofa and the chair were these wooden accents. And there was this one accent on the chair that kept coming loose. And when I was a tiny mammal, I kept pulling it out. Eventually, Dad glued this accent back on the chair with his hot glue gun.

Dad wasn't a crafter, so why he had a hot glue gun I'll never know.

To be fair, Dad worked at the furniture store where they got the sofa set in my very early days so I'm sure he used a juicy employee discount to buy it. It was still hideous, though. But I do understand the times and fashions were different.

Also in our living room, my sister Ivy and I had a kids' table. As we grew up, Ivy and I would eat breakfast every day at that table. We even had lunch at that table many days during the summer when we weren't in school. In fact, it was at that table where my Dad first showed me how to keep score of a baseball game. It was an NBC Saturday Game Of The Week featuring the Chicago Cubs and the New York Mets. And I'm pretty sure that Bob Costas and Tony Kubek were at the mic that afternoon at Wrigley Field.

The day Mom and Dad got rid of that thing was a sad day for my childhood. But it needed to go. Over the years this thing got beat up pretty bad. It turns out that kids can be abusive to cheap furniture. Who knew?

The carpet in the living room had this unique shade of red. Sort of a wine color - like a Bordeaux. And that carpet in front of the fireplace as well as in front of my Dad's chair (and make no mistake, that was his chair) contained loads of burn marks from either misplaced cigarette ashes or hot embers and ashes that popped out of the fireplace.

It's a miracle the house never caught fire.

That den in my little white house at the end of the cul de sac was perhaps the most influential room of my life.

Let's focus back on that sofa. That sofa was the site of my earliest vivid memory.

If I recall, it was hot outside. Granted, I grew up in Alabama where during July and August it could get as hot as the business end of a rocket engine. I remember it being especially hot on this day. In this memory, I was all of two years old. I was sitting on my Mom's lap on that very hideous sofa.

Have I mentioned how ugly this sofa was yet? It was like a grandma sofa but both of my parents were in their 20s when they bought that thing.

Okay, I'll stop talking about the hideous atrocity that was our sofa set.

My Mom loved reading to me. She exposed me to many of the classic little kids' books like *The Little Engine That Could* and *The Pokey Little Puppy*. Mom also enjoyed reading to me from news magazines and the newspaper.

I became a news fan very early. Hall family lore is that one of my first words as I was learning to speak was "Cronkite." I guess I always had an attraction to powerful voices with commanding presence.

Mom was reading to me on this sweltering summer evening. I'm pretty sure it was either *Time* or *Newsweek* because she was reading a story to me about President Carter. I remember seeing a picture with a pull quote and photo of President Carter.

As Mom would read to me, she was always engaging and inquisitive. She would ask me "what does this mean?" and "do you know who that is?"

On this night, something clicked. I'll never forget this...I started to read the article out loud to Mom.

I was two. I could barely talk by this point. But I could read. And this shocked Mom so much that I'm surprised it didn't trigger her to go into labor. She'd hold off on that until December of that year.

Oddly enough, this set me back when it came time to start school. I'm a professional writer. I've published two novels, this book, I've got a long history with the Good Men Project web magazine, and I've contributed to several collaborative books. I'm just saying, I write a lot of words and I'm pretty good at it. And to this day I couldn't pick a "schwa" out of a police lineup.

**

Flashing forward, this next memory was when I was maybe four or five. I mean, I was still a baby, but I had big boy underwear by that point.

Mom told me that it was bedtime. Ivy had already been put to bed by this point, but I was being obstinate. I guess I really was a little boy once upon a time.

Keep in mind, this took place on a Saturday night.

The bathroom was right across the hallway to my bedroom. There was a carpeted section in front of the vanity. That carpet...I wish I had a word to describe the color green that it was. It was like the marriage of goose shit and the 1965 Sears catalog. There was a giant vanity mirror, a bathroom closet where the dirty laundry was kept as well as keepsakes such as my Mom's wedding dress. In the area where the bathtub and toilet were, the floor was tiled.

For some reason this particular evening the tile was wet. It was probably because I just got out of the bath and Mom hadn't dried the floor yet.

Being the rambunctious little boy I once was before the world taught me that life was unsafe, I sprinted in from the living room. I hung a right turn into the bathroom, lost my footing on the bathroom tile, and landed mouth first on the front edge of the toilet.

I remember a lot of blood. I remember my Mom freaking out. And truthfully, I remember freaking out myself.

After the initial shock wore off, I found myself sitting on Mom's lap as she sat on Dad's ottoman. She's holding a washcloth with a bag of ice to my face to try and stop the bleeding and calm me down. I seem to remember losing a tooth that night, but it was a tooth which was destined for the tooth fairy's collection.

Mom went to go get my two favorite toys of all time - a stuffed Winnie the Pooh and Kermit the Frog. I was holding them as she tried to stop the bleeding. Those were two toys that were in my crib from day one.

It's maybe 10pm. Again, it's a Saturday night.

During these days, Dad worked nights. He was the manager of a bar called Cowboy, which was a country bar. And if you knew my hippie Dad at all, that was totally not his aesthetic.

I look up, and through bleary eyes from crying, I see my Dad coming in through the kitchen to check on me.

My Dad was the manager of a popular bar in a college town, and on a Saturday night, he'd left work on their busiest night of the week to come check on me.

Tony and Ann Hall were deeply loving people. They were generous, beautiful, and loving people with deeply tortured souls.

Mom was the oldest child of Melborn and Martha Ivey. She was incredibly close to her two siblings - her sister Joy, and her brother Eddie.

Mom was an intellectually brilliant woman. She was her high school valedictorian and earned two master's degrees.

In 1974, a graduate student named Ann Ivey Hall helped to open the doors of the now world-renowned RISE (Rural Infant Stimulation Environment) School at the University of Alabama. They began with six students, one teacher, and a teaching assistant. Mom was that teaching assistant.

RISE grew in notoriety in the early 90s when former Alabama Crimson Tide football coach Gene Stallings took a special interest and made a sizable financial contribution to the program. Coach Stallings' late son Johnny had

Down's Syndrome and spent a ton of time at RISE during his father's time at Alabama. RISE has grown and has been implemented in many large public universities nationwide. Mom always had a special place in her heart for the special needs kids who learned to thrive at RISE.

And she was there on day one.

The older son of Barney and Norma Jean, Tony Hall was a young child in Montgomery, Alabama right as the Montgomery Bus Boycott began.

My Dad was a gifted musician. He toured with several bands before I came along, but he chose to give up that life (thanks in no small part to some serious pressure from my Mom) when I came along.

Dad became an ace with anything that had a keyboard. From a synthesizer, a Hammond B3 Organ, a grand piano, all the way to a church pipe organ, he loved the keyboards. He was also pretty lethal with a flute. Their band covered *Stairway To Heaven* which he always loved to play. This allowed him a chance to bring his flute out on stage.

Dad's bands got to open for several of the biggest names in rock music history. One such event took place in May of 1973.

From the time it opened in the late 60s, through the 70s, Memorial (now Coleman) Coliseum in Tuscaloosa hosted some of the biggest names in rock music history. Santana, The Rolling Stones, and Elvis Presley – they all played the coliseum during her early days.

That's also the same building where I graduated from high school, but I digress.

The year before this story took place, Dad had volunteered as a student roadie at an Elton John show in Tuscaloosa's Foster Auditorium. This was right around the time when Elton's career was just starting to take off. Foster Auditorium became infamous for Governor George Wallace's "Stand In the Schoolhouse Door" a number of years before.

I've driven in Midtown Manhattan traffic before. And the traffic in Birmingham, Alabama's "Malfunction Junction" is the only mess that comes close to that chaos.

Long story short, Elton's bus was late. His gear and his band were in place, but he was stuck in traffic.

One of the roadies asked "can anyone here play the piano? I mean really play?" If they wanted the curtain to rise on time for the show, they needed to do a soundcheck right then. Dad raises his hand to volunteer. It turns out, he and his band covered a few Elton John songs. They needed someone to sound check Elton's piano.

The guys from Elton's band and Dad ran through the songs that Dad knew. The guys in Elton's band recognized killer young talent when they saw it.

After they got through a song, Dad heard some clapping from off stage. Dad turns around and sees Elton John standing in the wings of the stage.

"Sounding pretty good, lad."

Many years later, Dad told me that Elton's piano had the "sweetest keys my hands ever touched."

Back to Memorial Coliseum...

In May of 1973, Dad's band Brownwood had the honor of opening for an up and coming English band called Led Zeppelin. Brownwood played a short set, but by what Dad told me once upon a time, they killed.

Granted, while the crowd was there to see Robert, Jimmy, Jonesy, and Bonzo, the audience was appreciative of Brownwood.

Dad shared with me that John Paul Jones allowed him to play Jonesy's keyboard rig. He said their monitor speakers were so good that he could "hear a mouse fart."

When I was a teenager, Dad could tell that I didn't have some of the same taste in music as most of the other kids my age. And being the hippie musician he was at his heart, Dad saw this as an opportunity to shape me musically. And by that same end, shaping my own artistry as an author. And I'm grateful beyond words that he did.

Hello Again wouldn't have been the same book if he hadn't.

I'd grown fond of some of the smooth jazz music videos that VH-1 would play on Sunday mornings. You know, back when music videos on TV were a thing. By the time I was in sixth grade, I knew who Pat Metheny, Manhattan Transfer, and Tower of Power were.

By the way – just because Tower of Power has a large horn section does not make them a jazz group. Older me is still bothered by that. They are not Jazz.

They are a soul band playing soul music...from 1968 all the way up until today.

But I digress.

It was TOP that prompted my Dad to drop something off to me in my room one night when I was in high school.

"I think you'll dig this." Dad put a cassette in my hands. The front cover of this cassette was a giant pyramid with an Egyptian motif. The top of the pyramid had a brilliant light shining forth.

"Earth, Wind, and Fire..." At that point, I had no idea. I had no idea the magical journey I was about to take.

I popped that cassette into my Walkman and pressed play. I'd never heard anything like it in my life. The first song had a bossa nova feel with a rock and roll edge. Syncopated rhythms and radioactive horn licks – it was beyond the pale.

The second song I could've sworn was sung by a woman!

The cassette was the Earth, Wind, and Fire Album *All N' All* and to my ears and soul, it's the Elements at their finest. I was 15! I didn't know Philip Bailey was a man!

EWF means so much to me to this day, that I chose to title my first novel after an Earth, Wind, and Fire song.

After Dad first introduced me to the Elements, I walked into my room and Dad's old turntable was set up. I had a receiver and headphones, but no speakers.

"You like horns? You'll love this." Dad puts an LP in my hands. The cover features a stark black image with a mysterious woman in the shadows.

"Aja?" I had no idea how to pronounce it. Was it a hard J? Was it Spanish and pronounced like "A-ha?"

All this talk of Wayne Shorter, Steve Gadd, and banyan trees...I'd never heard anything like the title track to this album.

The next song after the title track is one of the most important songs I've ever heard. It's my song of triumph. It's my song of celebration.

Deacon Blues - my song of expansion!

After I received my author proof of *Written In The Stone*, that was the song I played at full volume as I cried for two hours. That song has also helped to celebrate Crimson Tide national championships, the Atlanta Braves winning the 2021 World Series, being chosen for amazing new jobs, as well as finding out that I passed my final exams with my Accomplishment Coaching program.

As I said earlier, Ann and Tony Hall were truly beautiful people. And for better and for worse, they've shaped me into the man I've become.

One Christmas when I was nine years old, Santa Claus brought me four tickets to see the Harlem Globetrotters play in Birmingham, some 50 minutes by car from our house on the southside of Tuscaloosa.

Truthfully, I may have cried when I opened that envelope.

I'd seen several Globetrotter games on TV the previous summer. They were a staple of ABC's *Wild World Of Sports*. I don't think I slept for a week before the game that February.

On the day of the game, I was the first person in the car. I sat in my usual spot - in the backseat on the driver's side.

As I'm waiting, I could pick up some weird vibes coming from the house. I seem to remember some yelling and some fussing and fighting.

Ivy comes out and sits beside me. She has a bit of a shell-shocked look on her face. But I didn't think much of it.

Mom comes out and sits shotgun. She's got an open beer in her hand and her breath smelled like beer.

Okay...this was the first time I'd noticed this...

Then Dad gets in and sits down to drive. He too is carrying an open beer.

Almost immediately, a heavy feeling came over me. I felt very uneasy and worried.

Against my better judgment, I spoke up...

"Dad, isn't it against the law to drink and drive?" I asked.

Dad thinks for a moment before he says:

"It's only against the law to be drunk and drive. Not to drink and drive."

This was the first time I remember either one of my parents outright lying to me. And it sure as hell wasn't the last.

Oh how I wish it was.

Chapter 2

The summer before I went into the fourth grade, my Mom and I took a short trip early one Saturday morning in July for a meeting at the Tuscaloosa City Board of Education building. And at this time, the City Board offices were in old army barracks buildings between University Mall on McFarland Boulevard and Northington Elementary School.

Before the mall and school were built on this site, it was the home of a World War II era VA hospital called Northington General Hospital. The ultimate demolition of which was filmed for a sequence in the Burt Reynolds film *Hooper*. This was all done before I was born, so I don't remember any of it.

But I certainly remember the leftover army barracks. The air conditioner was running so hard that you could store meat in that room. But I would never complain about things such as being cold as I was scared of every adult.

Every single one.

I was always a shy and quiet child. And bless her heart, my Mom used (or twisted) her special education background to convince herself that I was on the autism spectrum. Granted this was during the 80s and knowledge of the spectrum wasn't nearly as prevalent as it is now, she was convinced I occupied a space on this line.

Even well into adulthood, I am not totally convinced that I am not on the spectrum.

The test I took that morning involved questions and rorschach tests.

Oh, so many ink blots!

The test was inconclusive, but Mom was never satisfied.

I think I saw nothing but cows in those ink blots.

To fully tell this story, I think we need to go back a couple of years to when I was in second grade. Understand that I was still reeling from losing Joy and Carey just a few months before this. I didn't know which end was up. I had no idea which Mom I was going to get.

And yes, I will be sharing about what happened with my Aunt Joy and Uncle Carey in a few chapters. My Mom's sister and her husband died in the most unfair way imaginable.

I remember walking into Mrs. Smalley's class one day and she said we were going to have a pop quiz on multiplication tables. Immediately my stomach went into knots! I felt sick and dreaded what was ahead of us.

She dropped the papers in front of us and immediately I froze. I started panicking. And I may have started crying.

The quiz was to see how many questions we could answer in a short amount of time. Maybe 10 minutes.

I stared at that piece of paper and my mind went completely blank. I was frozen solid.

I think I answered 5 problems that whole time. And I got none of them right. So two days later, written in bright red pen at the top of the paper, was a giant zero.

My parents weren't angry with me. Even in the depths of their grief, they knew I got railroaded.

The next Monday, I was taken out of Mrs. Smalley's class and put into Mrs. Richardson's class.

She and I got along swimmingly, even though I don't think Mom liked her too much. Then again, Mom didn't like many people, including herself.

Yet this incident led me down a long and twisted road with math my entire scholastic career.

Words and stories simply came to me from an early age. I took to them like a horse to water...wait...like water off a horse's back?

Yeah, that's the simile. I could read at a fifth grade level when I was in the second grade, but numbers never agreed with me.

Back to fourth grade. Every day during that year, our teacher Mrs. Hamiter would read to us. I was just falling in love with words and stories at this point in my life, and what she did was like red meat to my heart.

During those after lunch reading sessions, a few of the students in the class would fall asleep. And I understand why.

But those words, the characters, and their stories, man...I was hooked like a bass on the end of a spinner bait.

Mrs. Hamiter introduced us to the Hatcher family. Our hero Peter - who was nine and in the fourth grade - was a good kid. Well-behaved and calm. This was before we met his comically and cosmically pain in the ass little brother Farley Drexel...but you can call him Fudge.

I inhaled *Tales Of A Fourth Grade Nothing* and all the subsequent books in the Fudge series at the time. To this day, Judy Blume is one of my greatest literary heroes and one of the few people in this world I'd be starstruck to meet.

In the class period before lunch that year, I'd go down to the basement of Northington Elementary School for my math class.

At Northington, they had these classroom "clusters." They had kindergarten and First grade classrooms in one cluster, second and third grades in another, and the upper grades in the other. And when we started going to different classrooms for certain subjects, we'd usually stay within the same cluster.

However, this classroom was on the other end of the school. This classroom might've been inside the school's steam pipe trunk distribution venue.

{Side note - if you understand the origins of that joke then you're my people.}

I walked into the classroom where I was one of three kids. And I joined this class well after the school year had started, so the other two kids knew each other well by that point.

Mrs. Shrout was the teacher. The class was fourth grade math.

I found math class very intimidating from the very beginning. Yet, when I was in fifth grade, Mrs. Richardson invited me back to her classroom to read to her students.

In those days, I didn't understand numbers. I didn't understand times tables. And I damn sure didn't understand how long division worked. Mom had me tested and I was placed in the LD math class.

Mrs. Shrout was an absolute sweetheart. She was so understanding and welcoming to me coming in mid-year.

And the other kids in the class were welcoming as well and we all ended up becoming friends.

But I never felt like I fit in with them. The other kids in the school would make fun of the kids in that class. One particular word was used on a pretty regular basis. All I'll say is that this word has three syllables, starts with "R" and ends with "D."

Do you feel me?

The other kids in this class didn't deserve this. They were sweet and easy-going kids. And I'm sure they have their own traumas they're working through now.

This "Math LD" label followed me my entire school life. I got special dispensation in any math class I had. I got to use a calculator - despite the protestations of anyone in the class. This led me to be singled out - and being singled out for that was the absolute last thing I ever wanted.

I even took a remedial math class in high school called Technical Math. I had a reputation of being a good student and nobody could understand how I was in this class. And even fewer could understand how I had permission to use a calculator. And the teacher's frustration with the constant questions about my calculator use didn't help my fear of being singled out.

The moral of this entire story is how I learned to make math work for me.

During my days as the voice of Eufaula High School basketball, I'm announcing a game at Charles Henderson in Troy, Alabama. At halftime, it was a big lead. I think Eufaula was up 31-19 at halftime.

One of the things that any good radio sportscaster does is give the score often. And it usually helps to give the score spread regularly.

And during that game, something clicked in my brain.

29-19 would be a 10-point lead, add two to get to 31, and that makes it..."The Eufaula Tigers are up by 12 as we head to halftime..."

I never carried a calculator to games I announced. And I kept my own scorebook. Counting up by 2s and 3s put me right back in Mrs. Smalley's 3rd grade class but without the meltdown.

Chapter 3

During my time in the Tuscaloosa City school system, some of my favorite memories were when we had "Bama Fanfare" field trips downtown to the iconic Bama Theater. Every few months, the acts playing the Bama would put on a matinee performance of whatever show they were playing for the local public school students. Provided it was a show that was for all ages, of course.

I'll never forget this one performance we went to when I was in fourth grade. We were seated in the balcony and we could hardly see the stage. But one didn't need to see the stage to feel what was going on.

The Atlanta Symphony Orchestra takes the stage. An older man with a distinguished shock of white hair takes the podium.

While this was a pops performance - they played orchestral arrangements of classic Great American Songbook songs - even to this day, I have never felt that sort of raw, unbridled energy. The energy coming from that stage could have powered Bryant-Denny Stadium for a Crimson Tide night home football game.

Touring Broadway shows, dance troupes, and the Atlanta Symphony were some of the things that started to shape me as not just a man, but as an artist, from a very young age.

The next year, in the fifth grade, we were at the Bama for a performance of a musical theater presentation. I was in the front row of the balcony seats. I wonder if Mrs. Moody could tell that I was falling in love with the performing arts? I think she could tell that I was hanging on to every second of these performances.

One classmate who couldn't give a flying honk about the Bama Fanfare performances was...let's call him M. Our friend M needed to use the little boys' room. He was seated in the middle of the row, several seats up from me.

When he got to me, I didn't acknowledge him. I was too wrapped up in what was going on down on the stage to let him affect me, you know, at all.

"Move retard!" Our friend M says. This got some snickering from my classmates and a rebuke from Mrs. Moody, but the damage was done. His nickname for me for the rest of the year was "Mr. Retardo Man."

I mean, M thought he was being clever because one of the big hits from previous years was *Mr. Telephone Man* by New Edition.

Sticks and stones may break my bones, but words land me in therapy over 35 years later.

One of the great teachers I had in grade school was Lee Gellington, my 7th-grade English teacher. Mr. Gellington was a small man with a massive presence. In a previous life, he was a Marine Corps drill instructor at Parris Island and still carried a lot of the mannerisms from his previous military life. While he didn't wear the giant hat that Marine DIs wear while they yell at you, he was very animated and demonstrative in his teaching. One of my favorite memories of him was when he would invite someone to "put some yeast in your feet and rise" to read a section of whatever work we were studying.

But it was in his class where I first got validation of what kind of skills I was developing as a writer.

We got to write different kinds of paragraphs, all the way up to an entire short story. And let me tell you, this portion of that class is one of my favorite things I ever did in school.

For the short story, I chose to adapt one of my Granddaddy's famous campfire stories called *Whumpus Cat.*

In my grandfather's story, Whumpus was this giant bobcat-type creature who lived in the woods and terrorized little kids who didn't go to bed on time.

And yes, for the record, Ray Charles could have seen what my grandfather was trying to do with this story.

I chose to adapt this story into one of a private detective Whumpus Cat who investigates stolen bird seed. I mean, this story had cameos from a couple of my favorite cartoons of the time - *Alvin And The Chipmunks* and *Inspector Gadget*. I mean, this story was damn good. Even as an adult, this story would probably hold up.

I got Dad to type it, and Mom was instrumental in helping me find the flow of the piece. But make no mistake, this was MY story.

A few days after we turned in these stories, Mr. Gellington sat down on the front edge of his desk. And he read my *Whumpus Cat* to the class in its entirety!

I remember feeling very proud, yet more than a little uncomfortable with the attention. And I also remember catching some bullying for that. In this context, I didn't care.

A dear friend of mine once said to me, "You know, that was probably your first ever 'author! Author!' chant."

I also got an A+...so, no big deal.

One morning late in April of my 8th-grade year was the closest I ever came to getting into a fistfight. That morning in the Eastwood Middle

School band room, I'll never forget it. And I wish like hell I could.

Our band teacher Mr. Hampton was out of the room, leaving the kids to do homework. What was he doing? Who the hell knows!

7th and 8th grade was when I started to gain a little weight. When you get the amount of trauma dumped into your soul that I got during those years, it's little wonder how I managed to put on a few pounds.

I will be speaking in great detail about some of those stories in this book.

I'm doing Math homework (traumatic in and of itself) when I start to hear two future felons of America start to laugh and giggle behind me. I had become so desensitized and dissociated during those days that I didn't pay it much mind.

This was before one of the felons physically brought me into the conversation that afternoon when he tapped my shoulder.

"We got a question, man," Felon #2 said.

"Yeah, what size bra do you wear?" Ringleader Felon asked. It should be noted that the Ringleader was already six feet tall and looked to be 21 going on 14. They were both laughing lecherously.

Never before this moment had I been brought to this. I was seeing red! My blood had come to a boil!

I shot out of my chair, got in his face, and said:

"What did you say to me!" But since I went through puberty a little late, I squeaked this and my point was lost.

Both Future Felons got up in my face and started laughing. I felt my life - and probably a suspension from school - flash before my eyes. I thought better of the confrontation and moved to the other side of the room.

**

In Tuscaloosa during the time I was growing up, middle school meant going to a different school for grades six, seven, and eight. This was challenging because of many reasons. All three schools were in different parts of town. You couldn't form any real connection with teachers. And you couldn't form any connection with the school building itself.

And high school wasn't much better. Grades nine and ten were housed in one building, and 11 and 12 in another. Yet for all intents and purposes, it was one school; marching band, athletics - both campuses were considered one school.

Confused? I know I still am. To be fair, a post-segregation Supreme Court ruling led to this.

Tuscaloosa-Central West Campus was right down the street from where I went to sixth grade. Those schools were on the complete opposite side of town from where I lived. I was maybe a month into my time in ninth grade when this incident happened.

I stopped by a vending machine to get a Coca-Cola to drink with my lunch one day. This was when these two girls approached the room where the vending machine was. One of the girls had a nose ring, but I didn't recognize it as such at first. Keep in mind, this was 1991 when this was happening. The nose ring was bright yellow and perfectly triangle shaped. And I seriously thought it was a shell from an M&M candy. Why she had a piece of a yellow M&M stuck to her nose, I'll never know. And understand, I knew neither one of these girls. I had no clue who they were. And over 30 years later I still don't.

I can close my eyes and picture them vividly. No clue who they were.

As I walked away from the drink machine I overheard this high-quality exchange.

"Who was that?" One of the girls asked the other.

"I don't know. I think that was one of them ugly girls," the other said.

I always loved marching bands - the Million Dollar Band helped me to fall in love with Alabama Crimson Tide football.

But...I played the oboe. I played that damn thing because I wanted my Dad to be impressed with me. As I was talking about wanting to be in the band starting in the seventh grade, he convinced me to take up the oboe instead of the sax like I originally wanted to.

Here's the rub, you'll never see an oboe in a marching band. The double reed mouthpiece is too delicate to take out onto the field.

To be fair, one of my musical heroes - "The Funky Doctor" Stephen Kupka from Tower Of Power - started on Oboe. But I never saw fit to pick up a bari sax. Or maybe I was scared.

Yeah, I was probably scared.

In 9th and 10th grade, I ended up becoming the marching band equipment manager at Central High School. This meant that I would be in charge of making sure the drum major ladders were in place by the time the band took the field, and passing out the plumes before the game. Plumes are the feather accents the members wore on their hats. I also remember having to help carry a portable generator for a live singing exhibition we had for one halftime show.

I share all this because I developed two pretty significant nicknames during my two years as the Central High School band manager. My nickname was either "Thunderhead" or "Captain Cranium." Y'know, because my head is big.

Truthfully, I became so desensitized to these names that I started to like them. I thought Thunderhead was kind of badass. But the way it was used, it was anything but badass.

When people call me "Rhyno," I find it endearing. When people call me "Ry," I find it sweet.

Not so much with the high school nicknames...

During the early 90s, the *Tuscaloosa News* ran semi-regular news stories or opinion pieces from students in the local school system. The first time I visited their newsroom was when I was a member of the *Falcon Flyer* student paper at Central High School. Our mascot is the Falcons, hence the name.

One of the first pieces I published was about former Bama football star David Palmer declaring a year early for the NFL draft. While this is a yearly occurrence for many college football stars these days, this wasn't an every year thing in 1993.

I wrote the piece following a tour of the newsroom. And at that moment I felt like I fell in love with the newsroom atmosphere. I wrote that piece on one of the newsroom computers that had a green phosphor display, heavy keys which made a loud "clack" with every keystroke, and other people's stuff on the desk.

"Do you mind if I take a look at that?" A disembodied voice said to me. I turn around and see a relatively nondescript-looking man looking back at me. Tall with an air of nerdiness to him. "I'm Cecil."

So this was Cecil Hurt, who was relatively early in his run as the sports editor. He was kind and generous with feedback, both on my piece and my writing as a whole. He was incredibly encouraging. Cecil passed away in 2021 after a battle with pneumonia at the terribly young age of 62. By the end, he had become an icon of college sports and Alabama sports journalism and was universally beloved. Coaches from Wimp Sanderson to Nick Saban would take his phone call at a moment's notice. He's a member of the Alabama Sportswriters Hall Of Fame. And we developed a relationship in subsequent years as he became a weekly guest on the sports radio show I produced.

But I'm embarrassed to admit that I didn't pay much attention to his feedback because I was so intimidated being in that newsroom.

**

My high school senior class of 1995 was huge. We graduated with more than 700 people. Total enrollment of both campuses was more than 2000 students, so it stood to reason our graduating class was big.

On the night of my graduation - I found myself feeling very little. I found myself feeling pretty much nothing. I can't help but think that I was simply burned out. Losing my Granddaddy, damn near losing my Dad, and damn near losing my friend Chris - it's enough to make one age way too quickly.

Yeah, I was the oldest 18-year-old anybody ever knew.

And yes, I will be speaking about all those stories later in this book.

Even during the hat tossing portion of the program, I was rather half-assed with my toss. I didn't want to do anything at all to call attention to myself. I just wanted to hide.

Now, remember the building where I told you that Dad's band once opened up for Led Zeppelin - Coleman Coliseum on the campus of the University of Alabama? Yeah, that's where our graduation ceremony was. Our class was so big, we had to have our graduation in the basketball arena.

Was it a full house? Hardly. But there were several thousand people in the audience.

We had a rehearsal the day before. There was a short set of steps that led to the stage. I found myself feeling incredibly nervous about tripping as I walked up those steps. This was a simple rehearsal so our principal Dr. Rhone could pronounce our names correctly and that we could get our seating arrangement correct.

Now understand, I was wearing shorts on the afternoon of the dress rehearsal. But I'd be wearing a full graduation gown on the night of the festivities.

The class wasn't in perfect alphabetical order. All of the valedictorians (and yes, I said valedictorians - everyone with a GPA of 4+ counting Advanced Placement classes was considered a valedictorian) sat on stage. And since I graduated with honors, I was soon after them.

None of the valedictorians gave speeches. If they had, we might still be there over 27 years later.

Eventually, our section was called to stand and approach the stage. I was third up out of the five who were honors graduates.

I find myself standing at the bottom of the steps looking up at the stage. Four little steps are keeping me from putting Central High School way the hell behind me.

"Don't trip. Don't trip. Don't trip. Don't trip." This was my internal dialogue playing on an endless loop.

"Ryan Dale Hall," says principal Dr. Rhone. Here's my moment.

One step, I'm good.

Two steps, still good.

Three steps, can I do it?

The fourth and final step...yeah, I tripped! What of it?

But hey...it was done.

When I started college, I was under the delusion that my life was about to become a lot different. I was under the impression that my life was about to get exciting, with a social circle, women, and happiness.

Yeah, no such thing.

The University Of Alabama was in my blood from the very beginning. It was in my soul. When you grow up within spitting distance from campus, it stands to reason.

I wasn't an athlete. I didn't wear the uniform of the Million Dollar Band. I wasn't on TV.

I went from feeling like a minnow in a crowded fish tank to feeling like a minnow in the Atlantic Ocean.

I felt like I was nobody.

It didn't help matters that in my days at Alabama that I still felt like I was emotionally stuck at the age of...well...high school.

I had some great educational moments while in college. I could probably devote an entire chapter to that whole experience. But the thing I wanted to close out this chapter sharing was a story about a woman...

We met in Journalism 101 - which was the introduction to journalism class that all freshman journalism majors had to take. She had an accent that was as country as kudzu on a slab board fence. She was also an accomplished clog dancer. She was from a tiny town outside Winfield, Alabama, and Winfield isn't exactly a bustling metropolis.

I want to ask you a question. There is no right answer, nor is there a wrong answer to this question. I guess this is what psychologists...and, y'know, me, call a hypothetical question.

When I said to her "Stephanie, I really like you. I'd love to buy you lunch tomorrow and get to know you a little better," what did she say?

I'd love to know myself because I never said a thing to her about it. I'd walk her to her car and have deep philosophical conversations about the world, the news, and her playing in the Million Dollar Band.

But did I ever ask her out for an actual date?

Oh sure, I pined and dreamed about it. But did I ever say a word? I damn sure raged out when I got home the day she told me she had a boyfriend (who she eventually married.)

This is a pattern that has been chasing and harassing me for as long as I can remember. It's still chasing and harassing me.

Steph, if you're reading this...I really did like you and I'm sorry for never saying anything.

Chapter 4

December 1, 1984

There's a Hatfield/McCoy duality within the State of Alabama. When you're born in the state of Alabama, you must declare. For those simply passing through, as soon as you cross the border, you must declare.

You must declare. Are you Crimson and White (yay)? Or are you Orange and Blue? If you are Orange and Blue then I offer my deepest condolences and my gratitude for reading this book anyway.

The State of Alabama doesn't have major professional sports. So, the Iron Bowl - the annual football game between the University of Alabama Crimson Tide and the Auburn University Tigers is the closest thing to our Super Bowl.

We take this stuff very seriously. In some cases, perhaps way too seriously.

Marriages have ended over this football game. Friendships have erupted into gunfire because of this game. People have been shot over a football game.

A moron poisoned trees because of this football game.

In the mid 1980s, Alabama was hardly the college football juggernaut they've become in the 21st century. They were in year 2AB (After Bryant.) And to be honest, the 1984 season was a bit of a mess.

Bama limped to the end of that season with a 4-6 record and their first losing season in 27 years.

Even though they had no championship aspirations, they came into the 1984 Iron Bowl with hopes of being a spoiler to Auburn's SEC championship dreams. If Auburn won, they were in the Sugar Bowl as SEC Champions for the second straight season.

Late in the 4th quarter, Auburn was driving and got stopped on 3rd down and goal at Alabama's 2-yard line. Bama led the game 17-15, so the obvious move is to kick the chip shot field goal where Auburn takes an 18-17 lead and make Bama win with a late field goal of their own.

Why Auburn head coach Pat Dye chose to go for the touchdown is a mystery that hangs over the Plains of Auburn close to 40 years later.

Auburn lined up in a wishbone backfield with two halfbacks and a fullback leading the way. Auburn QB Pat Washington handed off to Tiger fullback Brent Fullwood. The play was designed to turn the right corner - the short side of the field - and head to the endzone. But Fullwood got blown up by a Bama defender and forced out of bounds at the one yard line.

Bama took over on downs and ran out the clock, clinching the improbable upset victory.

Here's the thing, that was the complete opposite of how this play was supposed to unfold.

One of Auburn's halfbacks in that full house backfield was supposed to act as a lead blocker escorting Fullwood into the end zone. Only instead of leading the play to the right, he went left - the total wrong way! Fullwood was a sitting duck!

That running back who messed up the play was Vincent Edward Jackson - you know him better as "Bo." The next season he'd go on to have one of the most dominant seasons in college football history and win the Heisman Trophy. And later, he'd go on to star in those "Bo Knows" Nike commercials that were so prevalent in the late 80s and early 90s.

But on that afternoon, Bo knew going the wrong way, I suppose.

Bama was not supposed to win the 1984 Iron Bowl. And everybody who worships at the Church of the Crimson Tide wanted to celebrate.

Two such revelers were a young nurse and her husband.

In 1979 that young nurse married a handsome young man with a passion for

59

community theater. At the tender age of 32, the nurse had managed to become the head nurse at the Dothan, Alabama kidney dialysis clinic.

This young couple was my Aunt Joy and her husband Carey.

After the game, Joy and Carey climbed into their brand new 1985 Datsun 280-Z. It was an unseasonably warm day in South Alabama. They dropped the convertible top and they headed down Columbia Highway from tiny Ashford, Alabama to Dothan. Joy had a passion for fashion. So she and Carey chose to celebrate with some retail therapy and then cap off the evening with dinner and cocktails.

Columbia Highway is a long stretch of two-laned country road that runs through several small towns from rural southwest Georgia into Dothan, Alabama. Traffic can be very sparse, and it's mostly straight, so speeds can get a little excessive. Dothan isn't a large city. But the locals of rural Houston County, Alabama call a trip into Dothan "going into town."

A fun fact about Dothan. Their main road is called Ross Clark Circle. I swear to you, their main road is a 13-mile-long circle.

A driver attempted to pass Joy and Carey's Datsun while traveling at a pretty high rate of speed. The driver misjudged where she was, clipped the Datsun's left front side, and sent Joy and Carey careening end over end, tumbling into a ditch.

Joy was dead as soon as first responders arrived. Carey was taken to a nearby hospital and remained on life support before his Mom chose to end his suffering.

December 1, 1984...that was the day my joy, and my Joy died. My childhood ended on that unseasonably warm December Saturday in 1984.

I was all of seven years old. This was the first funeral I remember attending. The year before, my Grandmother died from a stroke, but I don't remember attending that funeral.

It was a double service for both Joy and Carey. The sanctuary in this old country church was packed - standing room only. This was the same church where my Mom and Dad (and Joy and Carey for that matter) were married.

As I walked into that sanctuary, two caskets were laid out. They were decked out with floral wreaths and a vibrant color photo of their wedding day. That picture was taken at the very altar where their caskets lay only five years later.

I remember holding my Mom's hand as we walked into the church. As soon as the four of us crossed the threshold, I remember feeling like my breath had been removed from my lungs. There was a heaviness and a sense of fear.

It was like God had given me a huge squeeze...but not in a comforting way.

Aunt Joy was strikingly beautiful. With dark hair and soulful brown eyes, she turned many heads in her day. An old family joke was that Joy was first runner-up in the 1970 Miss Alabama pageant...and I still don't know if it wasn't true.

Ann and Joy were incredibly close. While Joy was younger by a couple of years, the Ivey girls were inseparable. They were maids of honor at their respective weddings. While Ann was intellectual and shy, Joy was popular and outgoing. She was in a bunch of clubs and she pledged a sorority during her days at the University of Alabama.

She was quite an accomplished woman when she died. In fact, many in our family believe that if she'd lived, she would've gone to medical school.

Doctor Joy...

But it wasn't meant to be.

Joy and Carey had the coolest house...

One thing that prominently sticks out to me about their house was that their dirty laundry hamper dropped directly into their basement washing machine. When you dropped a dirty towel into the hamper, it fell directly into the washing machine. Unless the towel fell on the floor, which I imagine it usually did.

Joy's favorite color was sky blue. Their house (which was custom built by Carey's Dad) was painted sky blue. I remember their walls were painted sky blue. One could say she was obsessed with it.

Both Joy and Carey had an affinity for animals. Carey loved dogs. I remember they had at least two - one of whom was named Poco after the criminally underrated band from the 60s and the 70s. Joy got a lot of joy from her cats.

There was one thing about that house that I'll never forget. More than their Commodore 64 computer, their piano, or their really cool kitchen. Way more than any of the cool 1980s nerd toys that they had...

Y'all...they had a pool! That was like manna from heaven to a little boy! They had a diving board and pool furniture made from PVC pipe.

A pool, y'all!

I remember many brutally hot summer afternoons when my family would be down there visiting, we'd be invited to go for a swim in their pool!

And after we got done swimming, we'd be treated to Joy's world-famous (at least in Houston County, Alabama) homemade peach ice cream! What I wouldn't give for a bowl of that stuff today!

Or we'd get a slice out of an impossibly juicy watermelon. Which we ate with salt for some reason. And as I'm getting older, I'm finding that this is a thing...I don't get it, but it's a thing.

While their deaths were a terrible crime against humanity, that wasn't the greatest tragedy that came out of that day.

Nobody ever got the privilege to call Joy and Carey "Mom and Dad" and to me, that is an unforgivable and unpardonable crime...

I remember when I was a baby - maybe two years old - Mom was bathing me. I remember lots of bath toys. There may have been a foam tree...

The phone in the kitchen rang. This was the canary yellow wall phone with the curly cord that everybody had. That thing rang so loud it shook the house. It turned out to be Joy calling to check on Mom.

Mom left me alone in the bath. And being the precocious toddler I was once upon a time, I picked up the soap which was floating in the water. I haven't seen a bar of Ivory Soap in a few decades worth of Sundays.

Anyway, I picked up this bar of soap...and promptly put it in my mouth.

Mom comes back into the bathroom and she flips her biscuit. She wrapped me up in a towel and called poison control.

I was fine. But Mom sure wasn't.

Until the day we sold that house, I remember stickers from Alabama poison control EVERYWHERE!

I believe our family became rudderless after Joy died. In the subsequent years, Mom took this loss incredibly hard. I don't blame her, but I could feel it. She started to drink a little heavier. She began making some impulsive choices - like why in the world would a woman with hair as curly as hers get a perm is still beyond me? The 80s, man...

I don't think she cared as much anymore.

**

I've been asked by coaches and therapists from Alabama to Connecticut about what their deaths meant to me, my family, and how I am to this day. And it's actually pretty simple.

The most important lesson (and not one of those good lessons either) is that their deaths taught me that life isn't safe. That I am not safe.

I'm a pioneer. I'm a visionary. I'm a world-changer.

Yet the absolute scariest thing I do is to come out of hiding. Lord knows, this book is going to shatter all of that...

Because I have it that when you get out of line, take a chance, or do anything that is even remotely unsafe, you will get seriously hurt.

I was seven years old when Joy and Carey were killed. And after that point, I spent essentially my entire childhood in my bedroom with the door closed. I hardly saw anyone. I hardly spoke to anyone. I hardly did anything outside those four walls and that closed door.

But I stayed safe.

I didn't want to do anything that could get me hurt.

But I wanted to do so much more. I wanted to play baseball, but Mom was afraid I'd get hurt. I wanted to go out for plays, but I ended up talking myself out of ever doing that because I was afraid of the rejection and the hurt.

In recent years, I've made great strides in coming out of hiding. I've become a polished and powerful public speaker. I've developed a following and an audience on my podcast. And I had a blast taking an improvisational acting class and want to do much more.

But there's still a not so small piece of me who wants to stay hidden. A piece of me who wants to stay disconnected. A not so small piece of me who feels unsafe.

In a way, I guess you could say that I'm a 40-something-year-old little boy who just misses his Joy.

Chapter 5

When I was in sixth grade, like many kids around that age, I got chickenpox. But unlike most kids my age when they got chickenpox, I got dangerously sick. I believe at one point, I spiked a fever of 103. I was out of school for two solid weeks. And even when I went back to school, I was still not feeling 100%.

One of the most popular TV shows during those days was *The Wonder Years*. Side note, I was accused many times of looking like Fred Savage. Heck, even to this day I get that comparison. At least when I'm not being told I favor Jarred Fogle.

Yeah...that guy. I don't want to talk about that.

As I approached the end of my chickenpox incarceration, I was watching *The Wonder Years*. It was late April when I got sick so it was late in the season. And the temperature was starting to get warm outside so the air conditioner was on. This might've been the day my fever started to break and I found myself in my bed sweating like a pig.

I might have dozed off while I was watching TV. But I also knew I needed to use the bathroom very badly. I was a sick little man.

The bathroom was right across the hallway from my bedroom, maybe 15 steps.

While I was asleep, I remember this vividly. My bladder let loose a fountain of pee the likes of which I hadn't before experienced.

I was frozen in fear. I didn't want to move. I didn't want to do anything, but I knew I needed to get out of that bed. But my fear of moving overruled my need to get out of that bed. And I started to cry.

Around this time, my door opens and my Mom comes in to check on me. She saw my tears.

"What's wrong, Ry-Ry?"

"I had an accident." All the color left her face as she lifted the sheet and saw the lake of urine and sweat that had piled underneath me.

The next thing I knew, Mom and Dad were carrying the soiled mattress out to the curb for garbage pickup which was probably not going to arrive for several days. So my urine-soaked mattress was going to sit out in the mid-spring warmth to get moldy and funky.

And everybody in the neighborhood knew that one of the Hall kids had wet their bed.

To be sure, this was a small neighborhood, but the entire neighborhood knew one of the Hall kids wet their bed.

As I had twin bunk beds in my room (inherited from my Dad,) all we did was take the mattress from the upper bunk and move it to the lower bunk to set me up for the rest of the night. A few days later, Dad went to Sears to get a new mattress and we set my bed up properly.

The night that Mom discovered my mishap, something felt like it shifted in our relationship. I could sense Mom feeling more and more sorry for me. I could feel her pity.

But being 12 years old, I associated pity with love. And even now in my 40s, I find it difficult to tell the difference between pity and love.

Being the manipulative little guy I was, I wanted to use this to gain her affection.

But how?

After I recovered from chickenpox, I'd lay awake at night scheming and plotting and wishing this would happen. I would relish the day this would happen. I would welcome it and embrace it.

In my emotionally stunted mind, I thought that the day that I had to get rushed to the hospital with appendicitis would be the day that the people in my life would actually show me that they love me.

I'd be showered with attention and love and pity.

All because I'd be Mom's "little sickie-pie."

After Mom passed away in February of 2009, I medicated myself with food and self-pity. I was also drinking alcohol every night - going through a bottle of Jack Daniels in a little over a week.

I was also eating tons of sweets and gaining a ton of weight during the months after Mom died. I felt safe behind those extra pounds.

In late June that year, Dad, my uncle Alan, and I went to Orange Beach to see Steely Dan play in concert. The flashback scene in *Hello Again* where Jimmy and Mikey are at the Allman Brothers show and Jimmy starts crying over Derek Trucks' playing was a dramatization of this Steely Dan concert.

A day or two after we got back from Orange Beach, I got violently sick. I was convinced it was either food poisoning or a stomach virus.

I'll leave the details to your imagination.

I got better in a few days and was back at work for a few weeks.

Every Sunday night for a while I had the tradition of going to a movie. And this tradition had been going on for several years by this point.

A couple of weeks after the supposed food poisoning, I was coming home from one of those movies. It was one of the *Ice Age* movies. And admittedly I wasn't crazy about it. It was mindless fun.

However, as I was headed home that night I started to feel terrible. I felt like I had a golf ball stuck under my right rib cage. I assumed that some of the popcorn I ate had started to obstruct my colon. However, I got nauseous and had to pull over to throw up.

When I got home the nausea wouldn't go away. I felt like I couldn't stand up. And I was steadily getting worse.

I prayed to God that Dad wasn't too drunk to take me to the emergency room at 11 pm that night. I called him and he was coherent and sounded as if he was about to go to bed.

I knew I couldn't drive, and I didn't want to call an ambulance for this. While I still had the fantasy of being doted upon while ill, I didn't want to call too much attention to myself.

Ever the enigmatic riddle was I.

We got to the hospital and I'm absolutely miserable. This was the worst pain of my life up until that point. I was given a morphine drip and doctors ordered an ultrasound.

Yet despite the pain I was in, I found myself flirting with the ultrasound tech. She was listening to Dave Matthews when I came in. Dave isn't my favorite, but this ultrasound tech was very attractive.

Doctors suspected gallstones but they needed a little more testing to determine what condition my condition was in.

I was given pain management medication and ordered to my primary care doctor if my pain persisted.

Two days later I found myself trying to manage my pain by taking a hot epsom salt bath. But it wasn't working at all. So to the doctor I went. From there, we went back to the hospital where I was ordered to take an MRI.

"It's your gallbladder!" The doctor said with such glee as he came back into my room. I was admitted and rolled into a room and prepared for surgery the next day.

Dad and I got the briefing on what was going to happen. It was going to be a laparoscopic procedure with minimal recovery time. I'd be back at work in a week or so with minimal pain and scarring.

Yeah, no. Turns out that when they got inside they discovered that my gallbladder had become necrotic and had developed gangrene. It had ruptured and caused my white blood cell count to skyrocket. While I was on the table, Dr. Carpenter had to call an audible and he had to get the scalpel. I've got a lovely scar right under my right ribs to remind me of how lucky I am to be alive.

A day or two into my recovery, the doctor comes into my room and lays something heavy on me.

He told me that if you combine the infection from the rupture, my high fever, and the actual gallbladder rupture, the mortality rate was close to 60%.

"You're very fortunate to be alive."

After he left, I must've cried for two solid hours.

And I was alone.

Now, when I was 13, this was my dream. To be waited on hand and foot and doted on. This experience totally shattered that delusion and illusion.

During my time in the hospital I was threatened with a catheter because I didn't want to get up and pee on their schedule. I was woken up at 2 in the morning one night when I was there because - and I quote - the nurse told me "we gon' walk now." And then he fusses at me because I was walking so fast! I wanted to go back to sleep! You're not letting me sleep longer than two hours a pop! I just had major surgery and you won't let me rest?!

But the thing that breaks my grown-up heart was that I had two visitors the entire week I was there. I was, for the most part, alone.

I was harassed by nurses and was visited by two people.

**

I was probably 20 years old when I was first put on blood pressure medication. I took blood pressure medication for about 18 years or so. I suspected this medication was what kept me heavy for all that time. Combine this with the antidepressant medication I was always on, it's a little wonder why I stayed heavy.

I re-published my first novel at the beginning of 2022 with a brand new re-designed cover. The cover much better illustrates the mysterious nature of that story.

Yet I look at the original author picture on the back cover and I don't recognize myself. I don't know if I ever realized just how sick I was in that picture.

Starting around the 4th grade through my middle school years, a yearly event for school kids in the United States was the Presidential

Fitness Test. And the more that I started to gain weight, that made this event a living hell every spring.

One of the aspects of the fitness test that I remember the most was the "sit and reach" test. We'd sit on the ground with our legs splayed around this wooden box marked off with 24 one-inch increments. And the test was to see how far you could stretch. I always tested very well in this event.

We had this one gym teacher in sixth grade named Coach Dexter. He scared the shit out of me but I will never forget this one thing he said to me after I did this test during that school year.

"You do that well because your running is so poor." Yeah, he said it.

There were also things like the shuttle run, pullups, and sit-ups. But without a doubt, the bane of my existence every time this came up on the calendar was the one-mile run!

In sixth grade, we had these tennis courts and we'd run laps around the tennis courts to get to a mile. I believe eight laps made up the mile distance. And every lap we'd be given a small painted pebble to count the laps. And in my literary career, that is one of the most ridiculous sentences I have ever written.

But I digress...

I was feeling rotten on the morning we did the mile run. This was not long after I got done with my two-week-long bronchitis spell, so my lung capacity was non-existent. And even when I wasn't just getting over a respiratory infection, I could hardly run at all.

So I was desperately sucking wind. And I found myself walking way more than I could run. I was getting lapped on my left and my right. I can't remember if I even finished.

"Come on in," Coach Howell (the gym teacher at Westlawn Middle School who I wasn't terrified of) told me to come back. We were getting close to the end of the period and she didn't want me to be late for my next class.

The irony of this entire section is that as I'm writing this, I'm planning on hitting a good 2+ miles in the morning before I go to work. I grew from the kid who hated running to the grown-up who hits the pavement at least four times a week.

I'll never forget this time we were playing softball in seventh grade PE. I had my own glove and I was put in right field because the team that got saddled with me didn't want to put me in an important position.

I'm sure in modern-day baseball that Bryce Harper, Ronald Acuña Jr., and Aaron Judge would surely agree with this statement.

A popup got hit in my direction. I had a bead on the ball and I was so excited. I was so excited to actually catch something.

I had my glove in front of my face and watched the ball as it got closer and closer to my face...until, y'know...it hit me right between the eyes.

As the ball rolled to a stop behind me, I found myself stunned. I couldn't move. Hell, I might've been concussed for all I knew.

"God dammit Ryan! What is wrong with you?" One of the other kids started yelling at me. They didn't want to check on me to see if I was okay. They wanted to yell at me for reasons.

During high school, I started getting into weight training. I started to enjoy the feeling of a barbell on my shoulders and that locked-in feeling of a good-feeling squat. This interest in weight training continued all through college, though I found myself intimidated by the women in the student rec center gym rather than working out.

Few things do my holistic health more good to this day than a killer workout.

When I hit my late 30s, something happened. My mood leveled off, and I was able to wean myself off of hypertension medication.

I got into personal development work. I started working with a life coach - and became one myself (more on that later in this book.) I found friend circles. I quit isolating myself. I got back into therapy - and started taking it seriously for perhaps the first time.

I still enjoy getting primal in the gym with some heavy weights. But I also love flowing on the yoga mat. I have deeply gotten into running over the past few years and want to run a marathon by the time I'm 50. All I've got to say is this: 2027 New York City Marathon, I'm comin' for you!

Taking my mental health seriously, I have managed to get my entire health under control. I think for the first time, I realized that mental health affects my holistic health.

That's something a 13-year-old me who had fantasies of getting doted upon in the hospital couldn't say.

Chapter 6

I don't throw around this word lightly. This is a word and a distinction that I use on the rare occasion when it truly warrants it.

This is the time in our program when I tell you about one of my biggest heroes.

September 8, 1984

I didn't have many friends growing up. And what few friends I did have felt like they were simply in passing.

But that evening at Legion Field in Birmingham, Alabama, I met perhaps my greatest friend. A friend who has stayed with me through monumental highs, and deep, dark lows.

My grandfather had come up for a visit, as this day was also my Mom's birthday.

That morning at breakfast, Granddaddy asked me a question that would change my life forever. I believe to this day he had ulterior motives for the visit other than simply spending time with my Mom on her birthday.

"Wanna go to the Alabama game with me?" I didn't understand what that would end up entailing, but knowing that I'd spend the evening with my hero, I was all the way in.

We drove from our home in Tuscaloosa about an hour north to Birmingham. Granddaddy parked his Buick in some guy's front yard and handed him a $5 bill.

We started walking. And after what seemed like forever, I saw a sight I will never forget. Peeking over the horizon was a mass of gray girders with green trim. Thousands upon thousands of people were streaming in. Most of whom were wearing the crimson and white of the University of Alabama. Most of the people I saw were happy and were shaking crimson and white shakers with purpose and conviction.

But when we got to the stadium, it was like I'd died and gone to heaven.

When Granddaddy and I walked through the concourse and found our seats, it was as if a painting unfurled in front of me. The field was as green as any I've ever seen. The stadium was as massive as any structure I'd ever seen. The lights were brighter than anything I'd ever seen.

The voice of the public address announcer shook the foundation of that old building and sounded like God Himself. You know, if God had an Alabama accent.

After Granddaddy and I found our seats, here came the 400 plus members of the Million Dollar Band marching onto the field. And this was the first time my ears and my soul had ever witnessed in person the first five notes of *Yea Alabama*. I love the song, but the first five notes are heavenly.

I seriously want *Yea Alabama* to play at my funeral...

I didn't understand what I was watching. I couldn't understand why Alabama quarterback Walter Lewis wasn't on the field all the time. The Crimson Tide were upset that evening by Boston College and the eventual Heisman Trophy winner Doug Flutie. But God...I was a boy in love. I was seven and felt like I'd found one of the loves of my life.

My grandparents were longtime season ticket holders to Crimson Tide football games. In May of 1983, Granddaddy lost his beloved Martha from a sudden and massive stroke.

I discovered many years later that the ticket I used that night in Birmingham was Martha's ticket. That's how special that night was. And that only begins to tell you how special Melborn Ivey was and still is to me. And that admiration has grown in the three decades since his passing.

Granddaddy was an impossibly generous man. Case in point...two months later at the same stadium - Birmingham's Legion Field.

It should be noted that the Old Gray Lady on Graymont Avenue isn't nearly the cathedral of football that she once was when she was the "Football Capital Of The South" as the sign displayed prominently within the stadium proclaimed. Once upon a time, however, she was hard to beat.

That November afternoon, the Crimson Tide took on LSU. If you follow college pigskin now, Bama/LSU is one of the greatest rivalries in the sport. Those games regularly attract sellout crowds of better than 100 thousand people in Tuscaloosa or Baton Rouge, Louisiana. The Tide/Tigers tilts always bring in massive TV ratings. However, the game in 1984 wasn't even on television.

I don't remember a lot about the particular game. I mean, I barely understood what was going on at the time.

I remember my entire family was there that afternoon, except for Dad. I believe Dad had to work so he was unable to attend with us. It was my Mom, my sister Ivy, my Granddaddy, and me.

During the first half, storm clouds darkened the Birmingham sky like something out of a creepy movie. These clouds yielded a brutal rainstorm that saw the rain literally falling sideways. It appeared like the rain was swirling around that stadium. I'm not entirely sure a tornado didn't pass over.

My eyes had never before witnessed something so sinister.

The rain didn't stick around long, but when it was hanging out, it was in a bad, bad mood.

And in retrospect, the game was pretty nasty as well. LSU defeated the Tide that afternoon 16-14. That loss would clinch Alabama's first losing record since 1957 - the season before the legendary Paul "Bear" Bryant got the call from Momma.

Fun fact: Bama's coach in that 1957 season was a man with the impossibly Southern name of Jennings B. Whitworth. But everybody called him "Ears."

Why...who knows?

I'm sure it had something to do with his hairline...

That rain storm had us all soaked to the bone. I remember the stadium vendors were selling rain ponchos to those of us who failed to bring our own from home. And make no mistake, these ponchos were essentially Hefty bags with the Bama logo plastered on them. They were like barbers' capes.

They didn't do a damn thing to keep us truly dry.

After the game was over and we were all bummed out because the Tide laid an egg on the field, Granddaddy took us all to Red Lobster for dinner. I got my usual order from Red Lobster, popcorn shrimp off of the kids' menu.

Hell, I'd probably STILL order that if I could.

When the check came, Granddaddy reached into his wallet and shook his head. He pulled out a $100 bill which was dripping wet.

"I can't give her this," he says out loud.

"Daddy, just wring it out," Mom says to him.

Grandaddy simply shrugs. He stands up, takes all the cash out of his wallet, and wrings it out. What seemed to be a quarter cup of water fell to the floor.

"It's still soaked," he says.

"Daddy, c'mon..."

That's the kind of man that Melborn Ivey was.

Soon after the Japanese attack on Pearl Harbor, Melborn Ivey enlisted in the Army. After basic training, he was shipped out to the South Pacific theater and fought in the Battle of Guadalcanal. During that battle, he took an enemy bullet to the left bicep and was awarded the Purple Heart. For his trouble, he had limited use of his left hand and arm for most of his life.

After he got back home, he married his childhood sweetheart Martha and had three kids. The oldest of whom became my mother.

A fifth-grade dropout, Granddaddy was one of the smartest people I ever knew. He got into the family business and ended up becoming highly successful in farming and real estate.

By the end, he owned better than two thousand acres of farm and pasture land. He also had a feedlot where he owned a registered herd of Angus cattle.

In the fall of 1987, Granddaddy was honored with a national farm of distinction award. The awards ceremony was where he got to shake hands with President Reagan.

**

I was always a creative kid. I always had a huge imagination. On long car rides, Ivy and I would pretend that our Cabbage Patch Kids would trail behind our car in a spaceship and rain toothpicks and American cheese slices on the cars behind us.

And yes, the Cabbage Patch Kids dolls would unwrap the cheese slices before they rain them on the unsuspecting cars behind us. They weren't littering savages.

One of those long car rides was in July of 1987. We were out of school and we spent a good deal of time that summer in tiny Webb, Alabama visiting my Grandfather.

He'd just gotten remarried and I don't think my mom ever felt comfortable with his new wife.

For good reason. More on that later.

It was the evening of the 1987 Major League Baseball All-Star Game. I remember former Braves catcher Ozzie Virgil leading off an inning and scoring a run. Those runs ended up winning the game for the National League team that night.

After the game ended, Granddaddy asked Ivy and me to go with him for something.

We hopped in his 1979 Ford F-150 and headed to Glen Lawrence Lake late at night. This was a peanut field near where my former house would eventually be built.

He had these long irrigation rigs fed by water from Lawrence Lake. He had a patch of peanuts that were dying. And he suspected that he had a rig that had gone bad and wasn't working. Rain wasn't exactly abundant that summer.

These rigs were on a timer, and the timer was set to go off by the time we got out there.

As we were sitting in his truck and waiting on the timer to go off, Granddaddy leaned over to me and asked me one of the most important questions any human being has ever asked me.

"Have you ever heard of Monkeytown?"

I looked at him and replied that I hadn't.

That night, the lightning bugs were out in force. The lightning bugs seemingly came along with the sweltering July temperatures.

My Grandfather told a story that turned those lightning bugs into this race of alien monkeys. These evil alien monkeys had been sent to Earth from the planet Blinkatron for the sole purpose of sabotaging farmers' irrigation equipment. This was a worldwide conspiracy that must be stopped.

When I tell you that I fell for that story, I fell hard. I bit on that story hook, line, sinker, crate, barrel, earth, wind, AND fire! Maybe even blood, sweat, and tears.

I couldn't get Granddaddy's story out of my head.

About a week later, after we got back home, I still couldn't stop thinking about that story. I wasn't going to let it drop. And I was pestering my Mom the entire time.

"Ryan, why don't we write it?" Mom says to me. I always loved reading, but I never imagined that I'd be a writer.

One day, my Mom and I sat in my room for a couple of hours and worked on story ideas. In the story, Ivy and I would be child detectives who were tasked with uncovering the Monkeytown Crime Syndicate. And after we did, we were honored in a Rose Garden ceremony with President Gary Hart.

I'll let that wash over you for a moment...

Mom and I wrote the story. I did a few crude drawings. Dad typed it up. And we printed it and bound it in a report cover that had one of those thin plastic sleeves on the spine.

Granddaddy's birthday was in August. And when I gave that to him for his birthday, I think he cried a little. Not only is he the main reason why I'm such a massive Alabama Crimson Tide fan, but he's also the reason why I'm a writer. One could argue that he's the reason why you're holding this book in your hands right now.

After Martha died unexpectedly at the insanely young age of 59, granddaddy remarried twice. As I was only six years old when Martha passed away, I don't remember her well at all.

Wife number two was Mrs. Ivey for, I believe, four months. Her name was Ouida and she was crazy. She went on a redecorating spree once she moved in, painting every wall and changing every window treatment white. She didn't get to the carpet before they mercifully split. And she only managed to affect one room of the house.

The running joke in my family was that Ouida was Howard Hughes reincarnated. We don't know if she chose to store her urine in Mason jars, however.

In 1987, Granddaddy married a woman named June. And ironically, I think her birthday was in December.

June combined the madness of Ouida, with a heaping helping of mean and nasty.

March 1, 1992

I hate the phrase "chamber of commerce day", but Sunday, March 1, 1992, was one of those days. The temperature was an absolutely perfect 75 degrees. The sky was a perfect shade of blue. There was a perfect breeze.

It was a perfect day for father and son to take out the boat and go fishing. Dad and I didn't eat the perfect burrito for lunch, however.

We pulled into Holt Lake, an impoundment of the Black Warrior River, and dropped the boat in the water. Holt Lake is a reservoir that provides water for the small town of Holt, Alabama in rural Tuscaloosa County.

We dropped the boat in the water around 11. We got a late start that morning as Dad still worked nights in those days.

The fish weren't biting. And to be honest, I wasn't really feeling the water that day.

Something about the energy just felt dense and heavy.

**

1:30 pm...

I'm sitting on the back of the boat casting my lure, and I felt something incomprehensible to my 14-year-old mind.

I felt a heaviness come over me. Like a soul-centered heaviness.

I feel like I sunk into the rear seat of that boat just a little deeper. And I also felt what I'm pretty sure was a squeezing on my chest.

Not chest pain, but a squeeze.

I also lost my grip on my rod and reel. I managed to catch it before I dropped it into the water.

I'd done that before. And Dad was none too pleased with me.

Yeah, I once dropped a rod and reel in the water and didn't warn Dad about it until it started sinking.

I didn't think anything else of it at the time, but in retrospect, this was one of the most powerful and creepiest events of my young life.

Just a few minutes later, the feeling went away. The pressure on my torso went away. And I felt relatively normal and sane again.

7:30 that evening:

Mom made Sunday dinner - lasagna. She added pepperoni because she knew I loved that little kick.

We pulled in around 6:45 or so. Mom estimated that dinner would be ready around 7:15.

Around 7:30 that evening the phone rings. When I heard that phone ring, I got incredibly tense.

A few minutes after the phone rings, my Mom lets out a scream that could break glass.

"NOOOOOOO! I'M AN ORPHAN!!!"

Oh God...

I couldn't move. I found myself glued to my bedroom floor. I had a terrible feeling about what was going on.

Several minutes later, I heard a knock on my door. Dad comes in and sits down on my bed. There were tears in his eyes and all the color in his face had left him. The poor man looked white as a ghost.

"Ryan, I'm afraid I have some very bad news."

Earlier that afternoon, Granddaddy got a phone call about some people trespassing in a small natural spring pond on his property. This was a relatively common occurrence in tiny Webb, Alabama. And since it was a warm early spring day, instead of getting in his truck and driving down there, Granddaddy chose to stretch his legs for a relatively short walk.

After he was gone for about an hour - when this task should have taken less than 30 minutes - June got worried. She picked up the phone and called Granddaddy's nephew Lamar, who was also in the farming business and lived nearby.

Lamar gets down to the pond and finds my Grandfather face down, one hand clutching his chest, and the other trying to open his bottle of nitroglycerin pills.

He'd been dead for several hours. He was 74 years old.

In 1976 when he was 59, Granddaddy went in for open-heart surgery at Northington General Hospital in Tuscaloosa. This was the same place that was demolished for that Burt Reynolds movie a few years later. Northington was a VA facility at the time.

Remember the leftover army barracks? Those were left over from the VA hospital days.

Here's why I shared the story about the fishing trip that my Dad and I took.

Since Granddaddy died alone, the county coroner was called in. Lamar found his body around 4 pm that afternoon. It was close to 5 when the coroner arrived. I'm pretty sure the coroner was pulled off the golf course.

The coroner believes that Granddaddy died a little after 1:30 that afternoon.

Keep in mind the boat that my Dad and I were in was probably 240 miles from where Granddaddy died.

I will go to my grave believing that I felt my grandfather die.

I eventually ate dinner that night. It was probably after 8:30 but I eventually ate dinner that night. My hand was shaking as I shoved the fork into my mouth, but I eventually ate.

I wasn't a small child when he passed away. I was just a couple of weeks from turning 15. But I believe the year after he passed away, I managed to age ten years.

While it wasn't the grief - which was plentiful. It was a court case that aged me.

With his successes in farming and real estate, my grandfather amassed a significant amount of material wealth. He didn't include June in any of that wealth in his will.

To June's immense surprise, she was included in Granddaddy's will...but not in the way she was hoping. She wasn't named a beneficiary of a third of his estate. She figured she'd get a third - along with my Mom and my Uncle. In his will, she was provided a $400 monthly stipend for either the rest of her life or until she remarried.

My Mom believed while she didn't outright murder my grandfather, she didn't exactly help his health either.

Granddaddy's cardiologist prescribed a "bland diet"...whatever the hell that meant. I believe it meant easing up on the fried foods and sweet tea. But would you believe that every time we went to visit, June served fried chicken and sweet tea?! Southern staple foods, to be clear. But not good for a heart patient.

Turns out, June had been a nurse at the pediatrician that my Mom's family went to when they were children. Apparently that's how they met. June wasn't an ignorant damsel here.

My Mom was convinced that the only reason why they got married was so he could have someone to cook for him. And I don't know if she was wrong.

She sued Mom and my uncle Eddie for a third of Granddaddy's estate. Despite the fact Granddaddy's wishes were fulfilled, she wasn't satisfied.

Mom and Eddie spent a ton of time in Webb over the next summer probating Melborn's estate and dealing with the lawsuit.

In the end, the judge ruled in favor of the Ivey children. And until the day June died, Dad wrote and mailed her a check every month for $400.

Melborn and June got married when I was 10 years old, so my ways of the fairer sex weren't exactly keen. I'd argue that at 45, it still isn't keen. But I'm talking about 10-year-old Ryan here...

I knew what affection looked like and I never saw any affection between them. Not a brushed hand, a hug, a kiss - nothing.

The more I think about it with my adult mind, the more I think that Mom was right.

He's been gone over 30 years. And there's not a day that goes by that I don't wish I could call him and ask him what he thought of any of my books, or what Nick Saban has done for our beloved Crimson Tide.

Granddaddy was very human. He was very human and made human mistakes. And despite all of that, he's still my greatest hero.

Chapter 7

I grew up on a small dead-end street in the east end of Tuscaloosa. We had a charming little ranch-style house right at the end of a cul de sac. If I had any friends in those days, I'd simply tell them, "Yeah, just go to the white house at the end of the street, and you'll find it."

For my tenth birthday, Mom and Dad got me this basketball goal. You know, for the minute and a half I was interested in playing basketball. I never learned the proper mechanics of a jump shot anyway. Speaking for the slow and overweight among us, any basketball coach worth their sneakers would jump to have that on their team.

Oh, and I could barely jump.

27th Street East was just as much of a character in my life as the people in my life. I have lots of beautiful memories of that little street. And I also have some soul-shattering heartbreaks.

Imagine with me, we're taking a ride on a drone with a camera. This drone is parked right above our old street. The first thing you'll see is that the street is shaped like a basketball key.

Our house was perched at the top of the key. There were houses at both elbows, and all up and down both sides of the foul lane.

It used to bother my Mom to no end how often people would pop in for visits right around our dinnertime. She used to joke that our house must've been the social gathering spot at the Indian reservation.

As you come out of our front door and look left, there's a reddish brick home with reddish and white wood trim. This house belonged to quite an interesting couple - Mark and Carol.

I forget the sort of work Carol did. I believe she was a teacher of some flavor. I know that Mark retired from the Marine Corps. He was a Vietnam-era Drill Instructor at Parris Island, so you know he saw some shit. He still kept his military haircut and jogged many miles every week.

Oftentimes I'd be outside playing alone when he'd finish a run. He'd simply hold his arms on his head for a few moments to catch his breath before he went back inside to shower.

From the outside, Mark and Carol seemed to have an idyllic relationship. They would go out on date nights where they both dressed up.

To everybody's surprise, Mark and Carol got divorced when I was a teenager. Nobody ever knew the actual reason, but the suspicion is that Mark had a long history of physical abuse that Carol finally got sick of putting up with.

And turning to our right, we find the Townsends. To this day, the surname Townsend is a huge deal in Tuscaloosa business circles as the local Ford and Honda dealerships are owned by a family named Townsend. I don't believe they were related to our old neighbors.

When I was a child, Thurston Townsend had a delivery route for *The Tuscaloosa News*. He and his sons Charlie, Willie, and Tracy (or CharlieWillieTracy as my Dad used to call them) would load the newspapers into Thurston's old beige Ford panel van to deliver the papers every day. This was when *The Tuscaloosa News* was an afternoon publication.

I didn't know this until much later, but before Thurston moved his family to Alabama in the 70s, he was a prison guard in California. And one of the more prominent inmates he guarded was a young and charismatic cult leader and serial killer named Charles Manson.

A few years ago, Thurston's beloved wife Dean passed away. I believe it was Alzheimer's Disease that claimed her life.

One of my most prominent memories of Thurston was an incident when I was maybe six years old, and Ivy was in preschool.

Ivy managed to get something stuck up her nose and it freaked Mom out. But then again, even in her younger days, Mom was easily freaked out.

Dad was at work, and Mom called Thurston over to help her get that thing out of her nose.

The entire time they were working, my imagination went left. I flashed on that scene from E.T. where the authorities had to quarantine the house after they discovered the alien lived with them.

Side note: E.T. was the very first movie I ever saw in a theater. And it freaked me out tremendously!

The Townsends were lovely people and always good to us.

To the right of the Townsends' house, the old lady who lived there...she was a little weird. She always wore her housecoat. She never left the house. She was once spotted outside trimming her lawn with a set of kitchen shears.

Understand I grew up in the 80s. While this was well past the days of the Cuban Missile Crisis, the threat of nuclear annihilation was never not in the back of our minds.

This neighbor had a giant green fallout shelter in her driveway! Mom told us it was a "tornado shelter." But whenever we got hit by a tornado warning, we always went into our hallway. This fallout shelter looked like a giant green concrete igloo. I'd imagine the concrete was easily a foot deep. And lord only knows how much disaster food she had in that thing.

One of my favorite memories of that neighborhood took place in that backyard. One summer Sunday, a softball game started up with many of the folks from the neighborhood. Granted it was organized by the oddball lady's son who lived next door. Her son seemed to have it a little more together than Mom did.

During this game, I hit a home run. Yeah, I hit a home run. I'm a lefty, and I hit one the other way over the left field fence. It was probably only 80 feet, but I pimped it like Jorge Soler in game six of the 2021 World Series!

I think our neighbor Mike (and we will absolutely get to him) hopped over the fence to get the ball as it was the only one we had.

I remember one memorable Halloween. Ivy and I went trick-or-treating. I dressed as this astronaut cowboy hybrid thing. I've seen pictures of this, and so much of what I was wearing was covered in Aluminum foil. I remember this outfit, but I sure don't remember what I was supposed to be.

Anyway, we began our quest for our sugar high in the nearby Idlewood subdivision. This provided far more target houses than our little secluded dead-end street. And Ivy and I racked up.

After we cased Idlewood, we hit 27th Street East.

Most of our neighbors had solid candy stashes. The Townsends I seem to remember having red delicious apples, which oddly I didn't hate.

It was when we got to the crazy lady's house that things got...curious.

Keep this in mind, Ivy and I are both under 10 years old, and this lady was pushing 80 by this point. With such pride, she plopped a pack of Freedent gum in our pumpkin buckets.

"Is that denture chewing gum?" Mom asked incredulously as we walked away.

It was...

Down at the end of the street was a house that had lots of turnover. I think it was a rental property but I'm not sure. This house was rather nondescript, with white clapboard siding. And I also believe it was older than most of the houses in the neighborhood.

For about a year, this family called the Richburgs moved in. I don't remember much about the family, but I remember their daughter Mandy was my age. She was also incredibly cute and had this tomboy energy that still draws me in to this day. If they lived there longer, she could've been Winnie Cooper to my Kevin Arnold.

And before you ask, I remember what happened between Kevin and Winnie on the series finale of *The Wonder Years*. A boy can dream, can't he?

Now for the section I haven't exactly been looking forward to writing.

Mike and Sandy were always good to us. They became close with Mom and Dad over the years, and Ivy and I became friendly with their kids, Michael and Lisa, over the years as well.

Mike was an overnight supervisor at an area oil refinery, and Sandy was a local school librarian.

Their story is so incredibly tragic to me.

Mike was never one to shy away from his love of certain dark amber liquids that came in glass bottles. And when Mike was drunk, he was known to be a mean and nasty drunk. He was known to be quite the stern father even when he wasn't drunk, but the belt would come off at the drop of a hat when he was.

Mike ended up getting sober, which I think drove a wedge between them and my Mom and Dad. Especially my Mom.

Their son Michael was a few years older than I am and we became friendly over the years. One of the first times I ever got truly scared of guns was when I saw their family stash in their home.

He was a troubled guy. He fought battles with depression and self-medication. But by all accounts, he'd gotten his life together. He had gotten married and had a son of his own. But Michael's demons never left him. And they cost him everything.

Late one night, Michael became highly intoxicated and sat down in a chair next to his sleeping infant son. He stuck the barrel of a gun in his mouth and pulled the trigger.

I remember meeting Michael's son many years later when he was 10. I took him to a high school basketball game where I knew one of the coaches. It was so difficult not to talk about "your Dad" to him. The poor kid didn't know him as his Dad.

Lisa was a troubled young lady herself. She managed to become a mother multiple times before she turned 20 years old. She also stole money from me after my family trusted her to feed our cat Joy when we were on vacation one summer.

But back to Mike and Sandy. To this day, I don't know what happened with them and Mom and Dad. But there seemed to be this big falling out and I have heard from neither of them in years. They came to neither my Mom's nor my Dad's funerals. And to this day I don't know if they even know they both have died.

My suspicions are that the estrangement had something to do with Mike's sobriety and their hope for Mom and Dad to join them in sobriety. And knowing how vindictive Mom could be, this wouldn't surprise me.

Anyway...they were always good to us.

Chapter 8

During Ivy's younger and more formative years this became an annual rite of spring. Mom and Dad would invite both sets of grandparents, as well as aunts and uncles from far and wide to attend.

Our house would be so full of people that I'd usually have Dad sleeping in my bedroom on a small rollaway cot. I slept on that thing many times, and it was as comfortable as sleeping on a door.

And even in his younger days, Dad was an inveterate snorer. No sleep to be had on those nights.

This giant soiree was always on a Saturday in early May. I'd find myself grumpy that I was being pulled away from watching the Braves in an early-season matchup against the Montreal Expos. I swear it always felt like the Braves and the Expos were playing each other.

We'd all get in various cars and head downtown to the Bama Theater. Like many performing arts buildings, the Bama began life as a depression-era movie theater built shortly before the second world war. Before the advent of the Tuscaloosa Amphitheater, the Bama was THE cultural arts capital of T-Town.

The event we'd go to watch would be Ivy's annual ballet recital. Ivy was a regular in those dance classes for several years. At the recital, they would feature performances from all age groups, and perhaps a feature performance from either an advanced older student or a returning college student who took classes at this studio.

These dance performances were usually uneventful for the family's dynamic. Being the moody pre-teen I was, I'd usually spend the show staring up at the blinking star pattern on the ceiling.

However, this 1989 ballet recital weekend proved to be anything but usual.

For a couple of weeks before the event, the tension in the house was tighter than a guitar string about to snap. And I could feel every bit of it down to my soul. The volume of my parents' conversations started growing louder and louder.

The walls in our old house were paper thin and my bedroom was the first one off from the living room. So there was but one thin wall separating their conversations in all their dramatically loud glory.

About 11 one night as I was trying to sleep, this outburst roused me from my slumber.

"WHAT DO YOU MEAN THEY'RE NOT COMING!?" This exclamation roared from my mother's mouth!

Norma Jean and Barney Hall were my paternal grandparents. And I always found it curious that Mom and Dad shielded Ivy and me from them as much as they did.

Granted, Melborn had the farm and all the cool stories. Of course, I'd rather have hung out with him.

I never truly got to know Pop and Granny. And I never understood why.

Pop was a big, burly man with a receding hairline. Barney also carried with him a charisma that can't be underestimated. He was a natural leader, as he was a longtime manager of the Brockway Glass factory in Montgomery, Alabama.

Granny was a nurse. What kind of nurse, I'm not entirely sure. Again, I wasn't able to get to know this side of my family as well as I wish I had.

Granny worked for Jackson Hospital in Montgomery for many years. As a kid, I always thought it was First Alabama Bank Hospital, since the branch's sign was the only thing visible from the interstate.

Whenever we'd go to visit them, the energy in their house was always a little...wonky.

Ivy and I would share a queen size bed in their guest bedroom. And I seem to remember fights that we'd get into over who was closer to the door.

And they also had marble floors in their foyer. The coolness of which would never cease to interest me when I'd walk on those floors with my bare feet.

One of the few things I knew about Pop was that Dad couldn't stand his taste in music. If we'd get in their car to go anywhere, Dad would make sarcastic comments about this "easy listening garbage." And to be fair, it was lame. This was music that would feel perfectly at home on Lawrence Welk.

Oh, and Pop hung a tennis ball on a string at the front of his garage to keep it from hitting the front wall.

He was...that guy.

Pop and Granny were known to be from the "spare the rod, spoil the child" school of parenting. I can't help but think that Dad resented this tremendously as he and Mom prided themselves on never striking Ivy and me out of anger.

Pop had retired from his job at Brockway after more than 30 years. But Brockway's parent company hired him to go on a consulting job out

West. And they chose to take the leisurely drive from Alabama to Arizona in their camper.

They would still be in transit during Ivy's dance performance.

My parents were deeply offended - and rightfully so. Looking back on what happened with adult eyes, I feel like this was the culmination of many years of resentment from my parents. This was no isolated incident.

One of my earliest memories was of a boiling hot day one summer. Dad put his ID into a basket that was raised up a tall tower. This was the first step to visiting an inmate at one of Alabama's prisons at the time.

The inmate was my Uncle Alan, Dad's brother.

Yep, I had a family member who served time. I'm not proud of it, but it happened. He wasn't proud of what he did either, but it happened.

My understanding is that he got involved with the Dixie Mafia running drugs from South Florida when he tried to make a drug deal with an undercover officer. He was sentenced to seven years and served four and he was in prison when I was born. And if this happened today he probably would've died in prison.

This afternoon when we went to visit him (and I sure don't remember being in a prison) prison guards searched my diaper. And this was the last time we visited him in prison because Mom lost her mind about that.

I feel like Mom - and to a lesser extent, Dad - felt like Pop and Granny showed favoritism toward Alan.

And yes, I understand that he needed some support during the trial and the ultimate conviction, but something about it hit Mom and Dad sideways.

Granted, Mom was way more vocal about it, as was her wont.

**

I always felt tension in the air whenever we'd visit Pop and Granny. A heaviness that could only be brought upon by years and years of resentment.

I can't put words in my Mom's mouth. I wouldn't dare do that. But I truly believe that Mom felt like Pop and Granny simply never liked her. While Alan ended up being married five times before his death in 2021, Mom always believed that they showed his wives favoritism over her.

Why do I feel that way? I wish like hell I could ask her...

After the ballet recital incident, tensions in the house grew to an almost unbearable level. Mom and Dad fought seemingly all the time. And these fights usually bled over from the tensions that had grown from the Norma and Barney camp.

And God, I hate to talk about my own grandparents like they were camps in a war, but that's what it felt like.

A month or two after the ballet recital incident, the glass felt like it broke on a deep-diving submarine. And at 12 years old, I witnessed the entire thing.

We still had the merlot-red carpet in our living room. But it might as well have been blood, as angry as Mom was.

There had been some sniping back and forth between the camps for a few months. This was until a multiple-page, handwritten letter arrived from Montgomery.

Imagine this: 12-year-old Ryan, sitting cross-legged in the middle of that red carpet, watching the single worst fight his parents ever had.

And it was all about that letter.

Honestly, I don't think it was so much a fight as it was Mom verbally bodying Dad to within an inch of his sanity.

Yet, I felt stuck there. I couldn't move. I could hardly breathe. It was terrifying, yet I stayed the entire time.

And it was all about that fucking letter.

Mom ended up throwing that letter in the trash in a pique of rage. This was before she left the room and slammed the door of her bedroom.

After Mom left the room, poor Dad had a look on his face that felt so defeated. He pulls the letter out of the garbage and wipes off wet coffee grounds before he slips it inside a drawer in his desk.

**

"Ryan, Granny passed away last night." This was January of 1999 when I received this phone call from Ivy.

I was in my final year at the University of Alabama. And Mom and Dad had moved down to Granddaddy's house in Webb the previous year.

We wouldn't sell the Tuscaloosa house for another year or so.

The summer I was 12 was the final time I ever saw Granny. For the final 10 years or so of her life, we didn't see her. It turns out that Norma Jean Hall fought colon cancer for most of that time before she finally lost her battle in January of 1999.

While her official cause of death was colon cancer, I can't help but think that she died of a broken heart. Losing the opportunity to connect with her only grandchildren because of the unresolved anger and resentment, and the paranoia of an intellectually brilliant woman.

At the funeral, to say that reunion with Pop was awkward is an understatement. As an adult, being back in that house again was something I never thought I'd experience. Seeing people who claimed to know me, but I couldn't remember them, offering condolences to Ivy and me on the passing of a woman that neither one of us really knew.

The final decade of Pop's life was hell. He lived in an assisted living facility for a good portion of that time because of the Alzheimer's disease that eventually took his life.

The last time that I saw Pop, he didn't recognize me. He thought I was Ivy's boyfriend.

"Dad, that's your Grandson. That's Ryan!"

Pop eventually died in 2008. I was asked to serve as a pallbearer at his funeral.

It was at his funeral where I learned two important facts about him.

While we heard all about Melborn's Army exploits in the South Pacific, it was at Pop's funeral where I learned that Barney Hall saw combat in the Navy during the Korean War. Pop's casket was draped in an American flag which was folded and handed to Alan and Dad at the graveside service.

And it was also at Pop's funeral where I learned that Pop had a radio show. He played the guitar and sang in a rich baritone voice that reminded many of Burl Ives.

Barney Hall was the *Traveling Troubadour.*

We knew Melborn's entire military history. I even had long and involved conversations with him about his exploits in the South Pacific. Yet I never knew Pop was a Navy man until his funeral.

**

The computer I used to write most of my college papers was located in the "office" as we called it. This was a small room right off our kitchen. It had a couple of desks and a computer.

My mind started to wander as I was writing this banal paper about violence in video games. The professor claimed my writing was dull and I got a C on that paper. I can't help but wonder if he has read *Hello Again* since then? Dull writing...please!

Anyway, as I was writing, my mind started to wander and I started going through the desk drawers...and I found the letter! It was still stained from the coffee grounds that Dad wiped from it many years before.

This letter was easily 15 double-spaced, handwritten pages. I didn't read the whole thing.

I didn't think it was my place. There was this one line early in the letter where Pop quoted scripture.

"Therefore shall a man leave his father and his mother, and shall cleave unto his wife: and they shall be one flesh." - Genesis 2:24.

I skimmed to the end.

Pop's words are seared onto the back of my soul.

"For everything, I'm sorry. I'm deeply sorry. I love you. I will always love you. And I pray you will find it in your heart to forgive me."

I sure do wish I could have known them.

Chapter 9

"Ryan, what addict in your life are you choosing not to forgive right now?"

This question was one of the most intense questions I've ever been asked during a coaching conversation. And let me tell you, I've had metric tons of coaching in my life. In my coach training class, I had the most coaching in the room, other than my program leaders and the mentor coaches, of course. And this question landed like an anvil against my ontological skull.

My coach just looked at me and barely blinked. I was on the spot.

Do you ever have one of those smells from your past that you'll never be able to get rid of? No matter how much you want to, you can never forget that smell?

When I was a small child, my Dad's chair - the one with the hideous pattern and the wooden accent that kept falling off - had quite the unique smell. It was a smell I was used to, and it was a smell I accepted.

This smell was of tobacco. I shudder to think how many thousands of cigarettes that man smoked while sitting in that chair. I'm sure the number could probably give a team of horses emphysema.

Strangely it wasn't the smell of the smoke. My nose had long since become blind to that smell. It was the smell of tobacco.

There was always a carton of Marlboro reds sitting on Dad's end table. Also prevalent was a large crystal glass ashtray beside the carton of smokes. Dad preferred using those cheap, brightly colored Bic lighters instead of the custom-made Zippo that he owned..

This was a man who took great pleasure in sending cigarette carton labels off to get free merchandise. That's how he got his first portable CD player. He also got a denim jacket with a giant Marlboro logo plastered on the back.

Being around all this cigarette smoke caused me tons of respiratory issues as a young child. I had regular colds and I had bronchitis more often than I care to admit. And I'm sure that living with a human smokestack didn't help those matters at all.

One time in sixth grade I had bronchitis so bad that I missed two weeks of school. Nobody could understand why I kept coughing and could barely walk up a flight of stairs at the age of 12.

My cough was so bad that my chest was rattling. It felt like my ribs were rattling.

I was 12 and I sounded like I was a 65-year-old four-pack-a-day smoker.

I remember a doctor's appointment during my bronchitis incarceration. I remember this doctor's visit as being one of the rare times when Mom and Dad were both there.

I don't remember exactly what the doctor told Dad, but I remember him saying something to Dad about his smoking in the house and how it wasn't good for me.

Yeah, Dad wasn't too pleased with that.

That same summer I turned 12, I remember riding along with my Dad and his friend Charles to go fishing. Charles took us to this private and secluded fishing hole in rural Hale County, Alabama. And I seem to remember we caught some good fish that day.

But the trip back was no good. I sat in the middle seat of Charles' single-row pickup truck. I've got Dad on my right and Charles on my left. And they were both smoking like the Sistine Chapel during a papal conclave.

Yet I was scared to say anything. I didn't want to disrupt the apple cart. Until I learned to use my voice, this was a long-time pattern for me.

I have never nor will I ever smoke a cigarette. That's a habit I'll never pick up. Yet I've probably been around enough second-hand smoke in my day to cause some long-term problems.

By the time he passed away, Dad's lungs were practically roasted. He graduated from Marlboros to Black and Milds. And man, by the end of his life he was hooked on those little cigars. I'd see those stupid white mouthpiece filters on the ground. Even now that Dad's been gone almost eight years, I get a twinge of PTSD every time I see one of those filters on the ground.

"What addict in your life are you choosing not to forgive right now?"

I was in kindergarten. I found myself playing by myself in my room when I heard some screaming coming from the backyard. It was clearly my Dad screaming about something. I ran outside to check on him.

He and our neighbor Mike were drinking from small brown bottles and were clearly happy.

"What's going on?" I asked.

"The Braves just won their 12th in a row! One more is the record!" We were in the middle of April and I was close to finishing my kindergarten year.

"What does this mean?" I ask. Dad went on to explain that no baseball team had ever won 13 games in a row to begin a season. And truthfully, at this point, I was like - what is a baseball?

The next night, Dad sat me down and walked me through the game, step by step. And the Braves went on to beat the Cincinnati Reds that night 4-3. And while I didn't understand much, I became a boy in love that night. To this day I am head over heels in love with not just Baseball, but the Atlanta Braves.

And to answer the inevitable question, I cried like a baby after the Braves won the World Series in 2021. I'm talking about mad, hysterical sobbing!

I share this because one of the mainstay advertisers on most sports broadcasts is beer. And it's usually a never-ending battle for supremacy between Budweiser and Miller.

One of the things I noticed growing up was the changing can design on Miller Lite. I was always fascinated by how guys like Bob Uecker and George Steinbrenner would do commercials for them.

I remember asking Dad one time why they spelled it like "Lite." Dad gave me a patronizing answer, but I knew he didn't know.

I saw untold thousands of those cans in my house growing up. I saw the evolution of their cans from the spartan, mostly white, design to their current incarnation that's mostly blue.

I wouldn't drink one of those if you held a gun to my head.

Okay...I'm being told now that the can design is back to being mostly white. Shows how much I keep up with that particular beer...

Another smell that will stay with me forever is that of stale, spilled beer. Beer that would be spilled before throwing it in the trash, or a garbage dumpster outside Dad's bar. That rotten yeast and sugar smell is one that will stay with me for the rest of my days.

I am scared to think about how many thousands of Miller Lite cans I saw while I was growing up.

My Mom and Dad drank untold cases of that stuff over the years. Whenever they would get down to maybe one or two cold ones in the fridge, Mom would say "Tony, we're getting dangerous low."

To be clear, I'm no teetotaler. I enjoy a cold beer or a fine sipping whiskey from time to time.

But you won't get me to touch a Miller Lite.

Addiction stalks my family. It harasses my family. It controlled my family for years.

It's self-medication. My Mom and Dad did it. I believe their self-medication is why neither one of them are still with us.

I'm not immune to this. Not by a far sight.

My self-medication and my addiction has never been to drugs, smoking, or alcohol. One could say that I was addicted to food once upon a time. It's not nearly that simple. My addiction was to something way more insidious.

"What addict in your life are you unwilling to forgive?"

My coach asked this question several times during this one monumental session. Most of my coaching calls - as both a client and coach - have been done over Zoom.

I stared at my computer screen for several minutes. My screen, unblinking and unflinching. My coach, unblinking and unflinching.

Make no mistake, this was a shootout at the love and being corral.

My heart sank into my gut. My soul felt flat. I was about to expose one of my deepest and darkest secrets and I wasn't sure how I was going to not only say what I was about to say but how it would be heard and acknowledged.

"You know...I think it's me."

My coach jumped back in his seat and took off his glasses.

"Wow..."

Now I admit, there was once a time when I was drinking too much. My picture on the original back cover of *Written In The Stone* was a prime example of this. My face was puffy and bloated and I honestly didn't have a ton of life in my eyes. While I don't believe I ever had a problem, I was definitely drinking too much.

Lord knows how many calories three whiskey sours a night (on a slow night) were costing my waistline. I maybe only got drunk in public once. I usually only got drunk in front of Pete.

I finally graduated to old fashioneds. Though by the end, I found myself eating more of those sugar cubes than actually using them in cocktails.

The day that picture was taken, I was fighting with a little $50 point-and-shoot camera's timer, as well as trying to frame my face. It was in the middle of summer and it was hot as hell. I was sweating and I was stressing out.

I was wearing this yellow polo shirt. And I look down and find a giant coffee stain on it that I didn't know was there.

But yeah, it was there. So I changed.

The mere thought of doing heavy and hard drugs terrifies me. Getting caught and punished scares me. But what scares me most is getting hooked on that stuff.

I can hear the newscasters now...

"Author Ryan Hall was found in his rural Alabama home, dead of an apparent drug overdose..."

For a while, I was addicted to food. I was addicted to sweets. But not like cakes and cookies.

I was addicted to popsicles. I could eat an entire box of Blue Bell popsicles in one night and go back for more the next day. The sugar was killing me.

I have tamed that addiction pretty well.

But this isn't what I was talking about with my coach. I wasn't talking about an alcohol, drug, food, or sex addiction.

Addictions usually go deeper than just the rush of the high of the substance. Sex addicts aren't addicted to the act of having sex. An alcoholic isn't addicted to what's in the glass. A drug addict isn't addicted to the substance they ingest into their bodies.

The substances and the acts we're addicted to are not the reason why we've become a nation of addicts.

It's way more insidious than that.

I believe we're addicted to trauma.

In this context, I want to take a few paragraphs and speak about my friend Chris. He was one of my few friends from high school, and my friendship with him I believe defines what my addiction is about.

You could certainly say that Chris saw some shit as a child. When he was in elementary school, he was part of the hostage situation that happened at West End Christian School in Tuscaloosa, Alabama which made international news in 1988. Better than 100 people, the entire student population, were held hostage. The perpetrator was convicted and remains in prison to this day. This day of the hostage situation was also the day that Chris' parents decided to get divorced.

When we were in 10th grade, Chris got involved with some sketchy and dangerous people. His girlfriend was pregnant at the time, yet Chris wasn't the father. She was pregnant when they met. However, this girlfriend had Chris manipulated and gaslit to believe that he was the father.

It should also be noted that the woman was pushing 30 years old, yet Chris was 17. If you can believe it, this was only the mildest of their relationship complications.

A couple of years after they broke up, this woman became obsessed with having another baby, yet she had a hysterectomy after her last child. She befriended this pregnant teenager, took her out for a pizza one night, took her out back of the restaurant after dinner, and shot her point-blank in the head.

She cut out the girl's then-unborn child, and disposed of the teenager's body. She was convicted of the murder and was sentenced to life without the possibility of parole. In the mid-90s, this case was front page news in West Alabama and made national headlines.

The baby survived and was raised by her father.

While Chris and his girlfriend (whose name I refuse to use) were still together, Chris' mother got wind of the types of people that he was involved with (as she had discovered their already unsavory reputation in their community.) Jackie laid down the law. She pulled Chris into a confrontation while I was on the phone with him. And I heard much of this confrontation before I finally hung up the phone.

And while I say it was a confrontation...it was more of Jackie reading Chris the riot act. So...much...yelling. And I heard most of it. This left me with a really bad feeling in my gut.

A few days later, I came home from school and found Chris' sister Jennifer sitting on our couch. I didn't know Jennifer well as she was many years older than Chris. She was married and had a young child already.

"Ryan, sit down." Mom's words were anvil heavy.

Jennifer had an ashen look on her face. She told us that Chris was found with cuts up and down both forearms in a bathtub full of his blood. He was rushed to the hospital where he miraculously survived.

He was admitted to the psychiatric ward of this hospital for several weeks. I was given visiting privileges - I was the only one outside of his immediate family who had visiting privileges while he was there.

As I was let into this ward and Chris found me, he was on some pretty intense medication. I hardly recognized him as he had the energy of a toy poodle on a cocaine bender.

He led me into his room where we spoke for a few minutes. This was before I met Chris' roommate. I don't remember the young man's name. He was wearing sweats with no shirt. He had wet hair, so I assume he had just been in the shower.

But this wasn't what took me out. This young man was the first time I'd ever seen anyone with track marks from IV drug use. He was covered up and down both of his arms with track marks. And he wound up getting admitted to the psychiatric ward of the hospital.

I wonder what happened to that guy...

I only visited once. I couldn't wait to get out of there! That place scared the shit out of me. And this was before I saw *One Flew Over The Cuckoo's Nest* for the first time.

Chris and I haven't been in contact in many years. And I pray he's seeing a quality therapist to support him with the trauma he's experienced in his life.

"...what addict in your life are you choosing not to forgive right now?"

In another vein, I'm reminded of an old friend of mine named Noreen. Noreen, or Reen as everybody called her, she was a fascinating woman. I say "was" because she passed away from a heart attack back in 2016 and I didn't find out until a year later.

Reen's father was the chief of a Shawnee tribe in rural Kentucky. While her mother was white, she always identified as native. In fact, I was honorarily adopted into her tribe once upon a time.

Reen's Dad was also an alcoholic. She learned to cope and survive in the chaos that comes with growing up in that sort of atmosphere. Reen published a few academic works, but her passion was in fiction and poetry. She always wanted to write and publish a novel, but this was a task she didn't live to complete. Yet she always admired me and my artistic literary pursuits. I gave her an acknowledgment in *Written In The Stone* and she said it was one of the sweetest things anyone had ever said to her.

She gave me the perfect analogy for my family of origin once upon a time.

My home was full of love. We always had the basics - food, clothing, shelter. But our family became the cast of a play that changed at a moment's notice. We didn't know what play would run on a given night. Nobody gave out a script and we had to make it up as we went along.

And instead of an upbeat play like *School Of Rock*, it was usually a melodrama that Tennessee Williams would be proud of.

Madhouse Theater - running productions 24 hours a day, 365 days a year.

My addiction, without a doubt, is to the chaos of life. Unpredictability and chaos are where I feel like I thrive. I find myself attracted to emotionally unstable people and don't know what to do with myself if I find someone with a cool head on their shoulders. I find myself attracted to emotionally volatile women because that's what I saw in my Mom.

An alcoholic may enjoy the taste of the whiskey, but that isn't why he gets hooked.

A sex addict may enjoy the pleasures of the sexual act, but that isn't why they become addicted.

A drug addict may enjoy the rush of that bump of cocaine, but that rush isn't why they become addicted.

I was never addicted to the food. Food was an escape from the loneliness I experienced where I felt like nobody understood me. The food was simply the medication.

I'm Ryan and I'm addicted to chaos.

And it's a daily choice to forgive myself. Sometimes I fail, but the choice is mine.

My name is Ryan and I'm a gratefully recovering chaos addict.

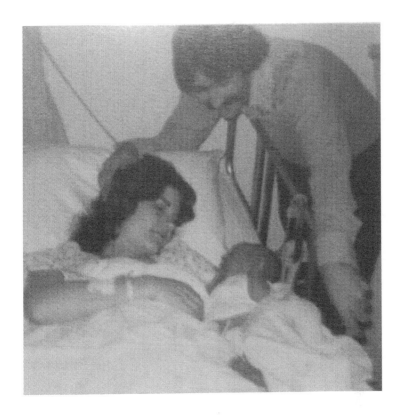

Day one, moment one - 1977

Memorial Day, 1977

L-R, My Dad, My Mom, Uncle Eddie, Aunt Joy

Kermit and Pooh - those were more than toys to
me. They were my safety.

Holidays 1980

I'm about four years old here. I remember once
trying to ride that dog - named Jason.

Mom and Dad on their wedding day - 1972

Dad and his band Brownwood. And yes, I stole that name for *Hello Again*.

School picture day - 5th grade

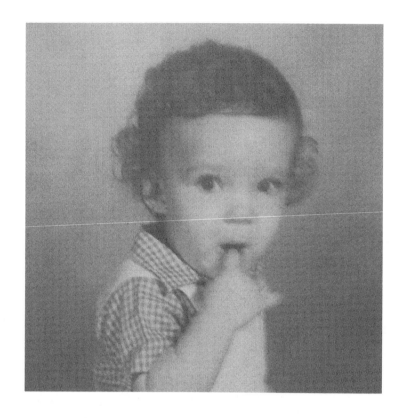

Baby Ryan - yes, that finger was tasty

Four generations of the Ivey/Hall clan in one
amazing photo.

Chapter 10

Aunt Joy and Uncle Carey left Ivy and me a significant trust fund in their wills. To this day, I don't know how much money was in that trust fund. From my understanding, it could have more than paid for my college education. Joy and Carey died before they were able to have children.

Ivy and I never saw a dime of that money.

February 5, 1994

I found myself awake at 6:45 on that Saturday morning. I was 16 and I had the sleeping habits of a depressed and moody teenager. Which meant that I would go to bed super late and easily sleep until after noon.

But that Saturday morning was different. I had a lot riding on this drab, overcast Tuscaloosa morning. I had been scheduled to take the ACT college entrance exam at 8 am that morning inside Ten Hoor Hall on the campus of the University of Alabama.

Shortly after 7, I stumbled across the hallway from my bedroom to take a shower. Even taking those ten steps into the bathroom, I could tell something was off. Something felt different. The energy was simply weird.

I also noticed that the doorway from the hallway to the living room was closed. That was my first tangible clue.

After I got out of the shower and got dressed, I walked into the living room and found Mom and Dad in the middle of a deep and intense conversation. This too was unusual because Dad worked in the bar business in those days and he was rarely awake before 10.

When I walked through the living room, Mom and Dad stopped their conversation to acknowledge me.

It was a cursory acknowledgment, no more than "good morning, Ryan. Good luck on your test."

This entire situation felt off. This entire situation felt heavy, intense, and terrifying. One got the feeling that this conversation had been going on all night and deep, deep subjects were on the table.

The visceral feeling I had when I walked into the living room that morning was as if I'd opened the window on a deep-diving submarine at a thousand feet deep.

The tension in the house that morning was completely crushing. And distracting as hell.

Not a good place for my mind to be when I had the ACT on my radar in a matter of an hour.

I managed to get to Ten Hoor right at 8 am. The proctor darn near didn't let me in the room. While this wasn't the first time I got stopped by a train at the Hackberry Lane crossing, this was the first time I ever discovered how irregular the train schedule was. How many times did that bloody track make me late for class?

As I was taking the exam, I found myself feeling distracted and worried about what was going on at home. I couldn't concentrate. I couldn't focus.

While my grades were more than enough to get me into school, the score I made on that exam was barely enough to get me admitted. Yet, still, I got in. I took the exam three more times, and I did worse on each subsequent attempt.

The morning when I was crazy distracted was actually the best attempt I ever had. Almost 30 years removed from that morning, I'm still shocked by this.

"Live from New York, it's Saturday Night!" Later that night, I was watching a random episode of *Saturday Night Live* in early February.

Patrick Stewart was the host, and I believe this was before he got "Sir'd."

My favorite part of *Saturday Night Live* has always been the band. Even when the comedy was absolutely unbearable, the opening music always delivers. SNL musical director Lenny Pickett and his sax are my favorite part of that show. Going to a live SNL is on my bucket list if only to hear that man play the closing music, A *Waltz In A.*

Right as future-Sir Patrick was making his way on stage, I heard a knock on my bedroom door. Understand, it was about 10:45 at night.

"Ryan, can you come with me to the living room? There's something I need to tell you." I don't remember ever seeing Mom this distraught before. All the color had been removed from her face. That same face contained a map of the world.

As this was the mid-90s, the furniture had finally been updated. We had a dark blue patterned sofa with a wine-colored recliner. I wonder what happened to those brown and beige atrocities we used to have. Oh, and the red carpet was long gone.

Mom's face was swollen and her eyes were puffy and red. One gets the feeling like she'd been crying all day.

"Ryan, there's no easy way to say this..."

**

The previous summer, Ivy and I had taken a trip with Dad to help him handle some of my Grandfather's estate matters in South Alabama. We'd kept up maintenance at Granddaddy's old house even while living better than 200 miles away in Tuscaloosa.

Ivy and I were going through some papers in the so-called "library" which was simply a small foyer that housed a bookshelf and tons of papers.

"Ryan, what is this?" Ivy showed me an open matchbox. And inside this matchbox appeared to be about a dozen pieces of rock salt. Why there was a matchbox of rock salt among some of my Grandfather's estate papers, I'll never know. Ivy asked Dad what it was, and he claimed that it was rat poison.

It wasn't rat poison...

The entire previous year, Dad had been acting unusual. He was prone to pretty nasty mood swings and bouts of anger. The anger was usually directed at Mom (of which I would hear all the fights.) These frequent bouts of anger and rage felt way too common.

As I was growing up I don't remember Dad having much of a sweet tooth. This changed around this time in our program. We were making a late-night drive back home from Webb. I had to be back to school because this was coming to the end of Spring Break. Dad noticed he was drifting off a little bit. Instead of stopping to get coffee (which he wasn't drinking during these times), he stopped at a convenience store to get an ice cream cone.

Mom was convinced his occasionally violent outbursts were related to "blood sugar." Considering how much sugar he was eating during these times, this wasn't totally out of the question.

It wasn't his blood sugar.

"Ryan, I don't know any easy way to say this. Your father's been addicted to crack cocaine. And he has been for a while." There was a leadenness to her voice that I will never forget. Her words struck me like a metal folding chair to the head. And there was a heaviness to her energy that gives me chills close to 30 years later.

Sitting on that sofa, I feel the weight of gravity pulling me deeper and deeper into that seat. My lungs felt like they were full of cement. My heart felt empty. My mind felt nothing.

I wasn't angry.

I was terrified.

But it also made way too much sense.

That wasn't rat poison in that matchbox.

His blood sugar wasn't causing his violent outbursts.

Dad's addiction was why Ivy and I never saw a dime from our trust funds.

This revelation about my Dad wasn't even the biggest blow I took that day. It wasn't even close to the biggest blow.

"Ryan, under no circumstances are you to let your father know that I told you what's going on." Well, there's something that hung over me like the sword of Damocles for many years.

I remember one afternoon I came home from school about six months before the crack revelation. As soon as I opened the front door, all the breath was removed from my lungs. Dad was in a very bad way. He was frantically looking for something in the filing cabinet in the office. Mom was helping but she was barely holding it together.

"Where is it?!"

"I don't know," Mom shoots back.

"Goddammit, Ann! Where is it?" Dad was frantic. He was sweating and freaking out and breathing shallowly. His face was red. I was scared he was about to have a heart attack right then. "I need it to buy change to open!" This was during the waning days of Tony's - the bar he owned for many years. And considering how strung out Dad was, no wonder the bar failed.

He was frantically looking for the title to his truck. He was about to get a title loan on his truck to "buy change" to open Tony's that night. I left the room before I learned if he ever found it.

It's readily apparent to me that he was either being hounded by a dealer to pay, or he needed a fix and couldn't get the money to pay for it. I knew that the "buying change" line was bullshit.

I fictionalized this story for *Hello Again.* Make no mistake, that story was as real as they come. And that was the single most difficult scene I have written in my entire career.

Dad never went to rehab. He detoxed in his bed. We rarely saw him for about a week. He said that Mom brought him food and water as he got that poison out of his system. They had to get another mattress because he sweated right through it.

And this was only what they shared with me. I get the feeling it was much, much worse than what they let on.

Years later, Dad said to me "I knew I was going to lose everything I loved. Your mother laid down an ultimatum. Either the drugs, or her and the kids." I give him massive amounts of credit for that choice. He got hooked on that stuff, and he made the choice to get off.

As I share this particular piece of our story, I want you to consider that this event took place around the same time that my friend Chris was in and out of the psychiatric ward after his suicide attempt. So my 17-year-old emotions were jangled, jambled, and sideways.

Seriously, I found out about Dad and Chris within a few days of each other. Less than a week!

One night around three in the morning, my bladder woke me up. So I headed across the hallway to use the restroom. However, I noticed something that completely threw me off - the light in the living room was on. The lamp on Dad's end table was on.

Dad was also sound asleep in his recliner. It was unusual to see him out of bed at this time of night.

A few clues stuck out to me as simply being off - you know, aside from him being passed out in his recliner.

The first was that the Nintendo that they usually kept in a cabinet under the TV was in the middle of the room, with the power cord and the controller cord trailing behind it. Dad got super deep into the original *Super Mario Bros.* during this time.

The next clue was that there was an open box splayed across his lap. This was a thin, shallow box that one might receive a shipment of business cards in. There was a good amount of marijuana in that box. But he wasn't rolling a joint or preparing a pipe to smoke (which was his preference over joints.) This box of weed was just sort of...there. Dad was rarely open about his marijuana use, even well into my adulthood. Yet, we could all see that he was smoking way more weed after he quit using crack.

Drinking more alcohol and smoking way more weed after he stopped using crack, you know his nervous system didn' t know which way was up.

The clue that really crushed me was what was sticking out from under Dad's weed stash. It was a handwritten note that I did not read but could make out a few of the words. Lines such as "don't want to live anymore" and "what's the point" dotted the landscape of the page. Was he planning on checking out for good that night? I'll never know. Not like I can go back and ask or anything.

Yeah, let's just say that I didn't get back to sleep after that.

**

After many years of therapy and coaching, I have what I believe is a better understanding of my Dad's state of mind during these years. And to be fair, this may be some of my issues and "stuff" painting this picture.

Mom gave Dad an ultimatum soon after I was born. "Get off the road, and get a real job because you have a son now." He chose to give up the touring musician life when I came along.

And I don't really think it was so much an ultimatum but Ann Hall reading him the riot act.

I truly believe in my heart that he missed music more than he let on. He missed stepping on a stage, playing the piano and singing. He missed making music with his brothers in Brownwood. In many ways, music was his identity.

He held onto regular "jobs" for a while. He became an entrepreneur.

But he never gave up that rock and roll dream.

**

Dad rarely featured live music at Tony's. Standup comedy was how they got on the map.

The Comedy Zone was a Thursday night tradition at Tony's. Steve Harvey, Bernie Mac, and James Gregory were the notable names who played Tony's when they were on the standup circuit.

The final live band they featured before they closed was called the Bama Band. The Bama Band was primarily known as the touring band for country music legend Hank Williams Jr. These cats were some heavy, heavy hitters in the Nashville scene.

It was about 11 pm on the night they had the Bama Band. I'm in the office doing some homework. Dad comes home frantically looking for something.

"Have you seen my flute?" The cats in the Bama Band had offered to let Dad sit in for a couple of songs. His energy was practically childlike. I hadn't seen anything like it in years!

That rock and roll dream never died.

Many years later, Dad and I got into the phenomenal HBO show *Six Feet Under*. This was a family drama that was set in a funeral home that won like 9 million Emmys. I'd come over to watch, the same as I did during the run of *The Sopranos*.

Before he became *Dexter*, Michael C. Hall (I'm pretty sure we're unrelated) played a character on *Six Feet Under* who was coming to grips with being gay in a relatively conservative family. And the episode I was watching with Dad centered on Hall's character as he got kidnapped and was forced to smoke crack.

The episode showed some of the frantic and euphoric experiences that one might have on a night smoking tainted crack.

Many times during this episode I found myself looking over at Dad. He looked so very uncomfortable. He looked like he wanted a safe to fall on his head. He may have even been sweating. And to be totally honest, I sort of wanted a safe to fall on my head as well.

After the episode ended, I sat at the edge of the sofa and took a sharp breath. My heart was in my throat! Admittedly, it was a terribly disturbing episode of television that I don't ever want to watch again. And I never have. I'd just spent the last hour watching a man who was having a fictional manic episode on a crack cocaine binge. But I was watching this episode with a man who assuredly had those episodes in real life.

Dad takes the remote and turns the TV off. He looks at me and smiles a world-weary smile.

"Ryan, I'm sorry. I really am." He then steps outside to smoke a cigarette.

Chapter 11

In 1983 when I was six years old, my grandmother passed away unexpectedly. Martha Ivey was only 59 when she suffered a massive stroke. And since I was only six years old when she died, I wasn't able to get to know her well at all.

While Grandmamma's passing was the first time I'd experienced the death of a family member, I don't remember her funeral. Ivy and I stayed with Pop and Granny in Montgomery while Mom and Dad attended her funeral. Lord only knows why Mom didn't want us going.

Mom took Martha's death quite hard as you can imagine. My memory of the immediate aftermath of her passing is sketchy. However, I do remember one thing quite vividly. Every night when Mom would put me to bed, she'd ask me to "say goodnight to Grandmamma."

And every night I'd look skyward and I'd say "Goodnight Grandmamma. I love you." For a year or so, this was my concept of heaven. It's as if we'd look up and my grandmother would be looking down at us while she was sitting on a cloud.

One night the following summer, I was lying in bed trying to fall asleep. While I was only seven, my mind felt rather adult during those days. And my mind could get dark quickly.

As I drifted off to sleep, I saw something with crystal clarity in my mind's eye. I could see my Grandmother's body lying in the casket. It was as if her casket had become transparent plexiglass. In my dream, not only could I see through her casket, but I could also see through the six feet of dirt. I remember seeing her lying there in her casket, peaceful and serene. But simply lying there...

**

As I shared in a previous chapter, my aunt Joy and uncle Carey were tragically killed in an automobile crash on December 1, 1984, about a year and a half after Martha passed away. I truly believe that was the day my childhood ended.

The following summer Ivy and I were off from school on summer vacation. Reflecting on this summer with my grown-up mind, I can see that Mom had fallen into a deep depression. My eight-year-old mind couldn't see how much pain she was in. I could see that Mom was sad, but I couldn't even begin to see the depths of her pain.

I could feel it, though. I think this was around the time when I started to develop my dry, witty sense of humor. This was to help her take the edge off.

This experimentation with humor led to me getting called a smartass more times than I care to count.

Oddly enough, I don't think my sense of humor ever helped her feel better.

One Saturday afternoon that summer, Ivy and I were at the grocery store with Mom. We might've been a bit rambunctious and Mom got embarrassed. I don't think we were totally out of line. Ivy and I were just being kids. This loudness and rambunctiousness continued when we got home.

Mom must've been in a terribly dark place that day. After we got home, Mom snapped. She started yelling and sent us to our rooms. Keep in mind that my room was the first one off the living room. This meant there was only one wall protecting me from what happened.

Mom was clearly screaming and crying from anger. And after a few minutes of this, she does something that I'll never forget. And I wish like hell I could.

She screams this at the top of her lungs in a tone of voice that felt like it was from outside of her body.

"GOD DAMN YOU BOTH!!!"

Mom's words and her energy hit like a sledgehammer to my gut. I've got the door closed and locked and I'm crying. I'm afraid that my world is about to come tumbling down on my head like something very heavy and dramatic. Similes aren't my specialty.

At that moment, every cell in my body was scared of my own mother.

"God damn you both!" I feel as if my mother just cursed God because I was born.

**

We used to belong to this church in Tuscaloosa that recently closed, Hargrove Memorial Methodist Church. It's a crying shame that place closed because I believe that was the last place I ever saw God as anything but a vindictive son of a bitch.

That last sentence, I will absolutely be expanding on that.

The pastor of this church at the time was a man named Ken Chapman. A kind and gentle man, he has left the ministry, earned his Ph.D., and now runs a leadership consulting company in Tuscaloosa.

Something that Ken did during his services was he'd call down the kids in the church for story time and discussion. I think this was a way to help our confidence as well as to get us more involved with the services.

Or it might've just been a Methodist thing, I don't know.

I can't remember why we had a falling out with Hargrove church. I'm sure it had something to do with my Mom's neurotic mind.

Growing up in the buckle of the bible belt, I was taught a black and white way of believing in the spirit world. God was supposed to be admired, revered, and we were supposed to kiss His ass every Sunday from 11 to noon. And then once a month we were supposed to eat potluck lunch afterward and kiss God's ass more.

Those potlucks were...well, they were a thing. At least one old lady would - without fail - would bring that weird ambrosia salad that had fruit mixed in with marshmallows and what I'm pretty sure was mucus.

And dear reader, this marks my third book where I've made a joke about that stuff. That stuff must've made quite the impression on me even though I don't think I have ever eaten a bite of it.

The way I saw it, from the time I was 7 to the time I was 17, so much of my world was wiped out by God. A "loving and peaceful God" saw fit to shake my entire world.

He killed my Grandmother, Joy and Carey, my Grandfather, hooked my Dad on crack, and almost killed my friend Chris. This was my life during those ten years.

After taking that sort of beating from a just and loving God, I had to ask: what kind of Stockholm Syndrome sufferer would trust ANYTHING after getting shit upon like that?

Just and loving, my ass.

Yet still, I hung on, if only by a hair. I hung on to minuscule amounts of hope and faith that God would help me.

That hope and faith were shattered one March night in 2002.

For a little over a year, I lived in the tiny city of Eufaula, Alabama. I was the news and sports director of a radio station called "Lake 98." They played classic country music...for reasons passing understanding. And by classic country music, I'm not talking about Hank Williams Jr. and Garth Brooks. I'm talking about Roy Acuff and Minnie Pearl here! Let's just say their version of *Smoke On The Water* was NOT the Deep Purple song!

During my year at Lake 98, I was also the play-by-play announcer for Eufaula High School football and basketball. Truthfully, this was the only part of that job I enjoyed and had any passion for.

During basketball season, this meant tons and tons of travel. I made many late-night drives from random places in Southeast Alabama after a basketball game. I'd get home at 10:30 or so, and had to be up and at the station by five the next morning to write my news copy for the seven AM airtime for my first newscast.

I received a late-night phone call on a rare off night. And full disclosure, my phone rarely rang. My social life was nonexistent.

On the other end was an upset Ivy.

"Uncle Eddie has passed away."

Ed Ivey was my Mom's lone remaining family of origin member. And one could argue that she too died on that March Thursday. Her body hung on another few years, but her spirit was gone.

Let's get one important fact out of the way: Uncle Ed was gay. This was accepted and honored in our family. Yet in Southeast Alabama, even in 2002, this wasn't quite as honored as it would be today. While Ed had been quite promiscuous as a younger man, he'd been in a relationship with his partner Wayne for close to ten years by the time he died. There was even an HIV scare that proved to be false.

But then again, that could've been Ed trying to get attention. He did that a lot.

Another thing that was well known and public in our family was Ed's love of and addiction to cocaine. In South Florida in the 80s and 90s, that stuff flowed like cake flour so no wonder he wound up getting hooked.

A ruptured aorta is what took Ed from us. While it wasn't proven, I believe that his longtime cocaine use is what exacerbated this. But then again, I didn't fail out of medical school because I didn't GO to medical school.

I say this to set up some context for the next thing I wanted to share. I saw this as the final heel turn for the man upstairs.

After I got the call that Eddie had passed away, I got in my truck and went home to Webb. It was a 45-minute drive that I made in not quite 35.

I stayed at Mom's and Dad's place for a few days to take care of their dogs. There was a memorial service in Ft. Lauderdale that Mom and Dad drove to. And then a couple of weeks later, we'd have a local memorial service.

The Ft. Lauderdale service was by all accounts truly beautiful. Wayne gave a eulogy, as did one of his colleagues at the college where Ed was a professor of interior design. The main officiant was a monk friend of his. There was also a performance of *Somewhere Over The Rainbow* by the South Florida Lambda Chorale. The Lambda Chorale is an LGBT vocal group to which Ed belonged and sang with before he passed away.

Ed's body was cremated as per his wishes. Since there was no local South Alabama funeral home to handle the arrangements of the memorial service, poor Dad got tasked with making these arrangements.

We had a terribly difficult time securing a member of the clergy to speak at the service. Some time conflicts precluded a couple of candidates from performing the service at 11 am on a Wednesday.

Dad was getting frustrated and called the pastor at the church where Mom and Dad got married many moons ago. The same pastor that performed their wedding had long since left that church and might have even passed away.

Mom was dead set against having this pastor speak at her brother's memorial service but Dad felt like he was running out of options.

After Dad gets off the phone he walks back into our living room with a shell-shocked look on his face.

"What did he say?" Mom asked. Mom was barely holding things together.

"He said he'd be honored to perform the service, but that he wouldn't be able to preach him into Heaven." Mom immediately got up and left the room and I don't blame her.

How could a so-called man of God be so callous? To say something like that to a grieving family...are you kidding me?!

Eddie had his issues and struggles. He struggled for years to understand himself. He struggled to accept and understand his sexuality. He struggled with substances. And he struggled with low self-esteem.

Make no mistake, he was a beautiful man. Eddie would've given you the shirt off his back. He adored animals. He was devoted to his dog, an award-winning Chow-Chow named Chaka! He had a special gift with watercolors and he hand-created stunning handmade quilts!

We finally managed to get a pastor from a nearby Unitarian Church to make the short drive and perform the service. As our family has traces of Creek and Cherokee ancestry, Ed developed an interest in Native spirituality. An interest that I have since picked up. This Unitarian pastor read a Native American translation of the 23rd Psalm that was truly breathtaking. I kept a copy of that passage in my wallet for several years.

In the years since this incident, I developed the opinion that religious people were weak and brainwashed. I wondered many times how anyone could possibly be that weak-willed?

"I trust in God." You trust in a being who could stick a rusty piece of rebar where the sun don't shine and not use lubrication. A God who would do this with a smile on his omnipotent face?

"Ryan, what are your thoughts on God?" I was once asked on a first date. I'll never forget that one. A FIRST date!

"Whatever brings me peace." She was...let's just call it underwhelmed by that answer. There wasn't a second date until several months later and even that ended in disaster.

The final straw was the day before my Mom passed away.

Mom held on for several days in the CCU. She was in total liver failure when they brought her to the hospital. Her skin was jaundiced and she was carrying around gallons - GALLONS - of extra fluid in her body.

Ironically, she died when she was 59. She was the exact same age Martha was when she left her body.

If you've ever visited anyone in an ICU or CCU, they only allow visitors at certain times. And between those visiting hours, they'd make people leave.

After one late night visiting hour, I wandered away from the waiting room. I wandered away from the stale coffee and the water cooler with the cone-shaped paper cups and the Fox News Channel on an endless loop.

A short walk down the hallway was a prayer room. This room had a Bible, a copy of the Talmud, and a copy of the Quran. There were a couple of church-type pews.

"What the hell?" I thought.

I walk in, close the door, and sit down.

I remember it being incredibly cold in that room. The air conditioner was on full blast. Why...who knows? It was February!

I felt like a total hypocrite sitting there. I was about to ask God to try and save my Mom, yet I truly believed that God wasn't real.

"Well, you got anything?" I felt nothing. "You just gonna ignore me?" Still nothing. "Ah, fuck this! And fuck you!" I walked out.

The reality of what happened with Mom was that her spirit died on that day in March of 2002. Mom had abused her body with alcohol, poor eating habits, and self-hatred for many years. And it finally caught up with her.

But to my angry and bitter mind, God killed her.

Over time, however, I started to see and feel some of the work that He was starting to show me. Slowly but surely...

The best example of this was in the spring of 2013. I'm sitting in the sauna after a gym workout. I closed my eyes and I saw something unfolding in front of me in my mind's eye.

We're in a remote barn somewhere in the middle east. I'm hanging upside down from my feet. And out of the blue, a bunch of Navy SEALs bust through the door to get me out of there.

I didn't know where it would go, but when I got home I sat down at my computer and opened up a Microsoft Word file and I typed this sentence.

"Oh hell. Here we go again."

If you've read my first novel *Written In The Stone*, you might recognize this story and that opening line. That afternoon in the sauna, the opening of my first novel simply unfolded right in front of me.

As the writing evolved, the characters started feeling a lot more real. The family dynamic in the Whitehead family started feeling much like the Hall family dynamic. Especially the character of Terri - Ethan's mother.

The way her story wound up evolving became a way for me to re-write how I wished my Mom's story would've ended. It became a way for me to heal my broken heart.

I know with little doubt that it was God who placed that story in my soul. And that story ended up becoming my first book and seeing a dream I had since I was 10 years old come true.

In the early 2000s, I had to move back in with my Mom and Dad after a series of job losses. I tried living a normal, well-intentioned life, but I still felt like I was a child in an adult body.

Unbeknownst to me, I was falling into a deep and dark depression. I was going out to bars more frequently and occasionally driving when I shouldn't be. I was gaining weight, despite the fact I was going to the gym practically every day.

I was falling down a deep hole.

I remember coming home from work one day and Mom and Dad were in the middle of one of their classic screaming matches. This was probably about my Dad's relationship with my uncle Alan. Mom couldn't stand Alan because he was influencing my Dad. She said it turned him into a "Hall Man" every time he'd speak to him.

Translation - Alan's confidence bordering on arrogance would affect Dad and this would make Mom's insecurity spike.

But this evening I'd had enough. The glass broke on that submarine and I desperately needed to get away. The energy was just too much.

So I got in my truck and went over to our family's lake. I parked near where my house would eventually be built. And ironically right near the place where Granddaddy first told me about the ballad of *Monkeytown*. This was right at dusk so the sun was barely peeking over the horizon. We're in the middle of the summer, so the humidity was bordering on stifling. It was still quite hot.

I'd had enough. I was sick and tired of living where I was living. I was sick of the job I was working - a call center job for an animal supply company. I was sick of the rejection by the woman I was interested in (and I could take rejection VERY personally.) I was just sick and tired of being sick and tired.

So I parked my pickup truck, got out and lowered the tailgate. I hopped up and sat down and took a deep breath.

"You fucking asshole. You love messing with me, don't you." I unleashed a string of profanity at God over the course of the next few moments that would make an oil rig roughneck need a fainting couch.

When I was done several minutes later, I was breathing heavily. I was sweating. My heart was pounding. I was completely and totally spent.

Off in the distance, I could hear a frog start to croak. Then another. Yet another. Eventually, it felt like there were hundreds of frogs croaking in a chorus. But the way it sounded to me felt like I was being applauded.

I looked down at my feet dangling off the tailgate of my truck and I saw a tiny bunny looking up at me. When I shifted my weight, it scampered away.

God and I have a long history of a hate/love relationship. But the older and more mature I become, the more I can see that God has been begging me for a relationship.

Slowly but surely, I'm learning to trust that He won't hurt me. But most of all, the relationship doesn't necessarily have to look one particular way.

Chapter 12

On April 30, 2022, legendary country music artist Naomi Judd took her own life after battling severe depression and suicidal ideation for many years. After The Judds finished regular touring in the early 90s after Naomi was diagnosed with Hepatitis C, she developed severe depression and anxiety that couldn't be properly treated.

A couple of weeks after Naomi's tragic passing, I watched a video from an interview that Ashley Judd gave to ABC's Diane Sawyer. Despite Ashley's public persona as a celebrity and an activist, in this interview, I saw a traumatized and scared adult little girl.

But most of all, I felt extreme empathy with Ashley for what she saw and what she must've seen growing up. Ashley spoke so bravely and eloquently about who she saw her mother be in public. She spoke about how she would know the names and the stories of everyone in the restaurant where they'd eat. She'd even know the story of the cashier at Walgreens. She was so outgoing and bubbly in public.

But in private, there were weeks where she'd never get off the sofa. There were times when she wouldn't even practice basic hygiene.

As Ashley's speaking about seeing her Mom's duality, I got chills deep in places I didn't know I had. I've seen this movie before.

I lived inside of this exact movie!

Only the part of Naomi Judd was played by Ann Ivey Hall.

**

Once upon a time, as a child, I remember my Mom being well-adjusted. And I remember that she had friends.

If you knew the woman who, by the end, had so isolated herself, you probably wouldn't believe me; Ann Hall had friends.

One of the earliest friends of hers I remember was this woman named Vicki. And if you looked up the textbook definition of an 80s stereotype, you'd probably see a picture of this woman. She smoked Virginia Slim cigarettes. And she kept them in one of those faux leather wallets with the brass snaps, with a Bic lighter stuffed in the pocket of this thing. Her husband was a high-ranking firefighter in the Tuscaloosa Fire Department and she smoked. There's some Reagan-era irony for ya.

Vicki was also rarely seen without a cold can of TAB. I once heard that Tab stood for "Totally Artificial Beverage." If you go to Snopes, you won't find a definitive answer to this.

But I'm not giving up on this hypothesis being real.

And lastly, Vicki always - and I do mean always - had a deep tan. I never saw her not looking like a well-worn catcher's mitt.

I remember when I was maybe five or six, Mom took Ivy and me to this place to play where she met Vicki. When we got there, Mom and Vicki went into this room that had loud music. This was a place called Nationwide Health Spa and Mom and Vicki went to this step aerobics class.

I remember this one time they had us over to eat dinner. After dinner, I went outside with Vicki's two sons Eric and Brian and played on their basketball court. Only Eric and Brian played one-on-one. I was the referee and ran aimlessly around their driveway court because that is what I thought I saw on TV.

Gradually over time, Vicki stopped coming over to watch *Dallas* and *Knots Landing*. And for the life of me, I don't remember why.

When my grandmother passed away in 1983, Mom didn't take that well. She still had her best friend and sister, Joy. She and Mom were thick as thieves and incredibly close.

After Joy was killed in that car crash, one could say that a little bit of her spirit died. She was never the same woman after that.

After Joy and Carey passed away, this was around the time she started self-medicating. She stopped exercising. She started alienating herself from some friends in her life. And she'd occasionally take out her pain on Ivy and me.

"God damn you both!" Remember that?

Yet still, she had friends.

This story must have been during the early 90s as I was in high school. My uncle Eddie was in town for a rare visit. He was living in South Florida at the time, so time and distance kept him away for years at a time.

While Mom always enjoyed having Ed visit, something about this visit landed off-key for me. It was as if the energetic balance of the house was simply off.

During this time in the early 90s, Mom and Dad were at an ebb in their relationship. Dad was gone a lot as he was still working nights during this time. This was also around the time when Dad's active crack cocaine addiction was ramping up, but we were in the blind about that.

Mom sat in the middle of my bedroom on the floor and leaned against the small Alabama Crimson Tide milking stool I owned once upon a time. While this conversation started off as a teenager confiding in his mother about some trouble in his life - I think the conversation was about a girl who wouldn't give me the time of day but I was in love with the idea of her (boy there's a pattern in my life,) it wound up shifting to Mom confessing to me about wishing she'd married her high school boyfriend.

Yeah, this is something that any teenage boy needed to hear. But being the good little boy I was and wanting nothing more than to take care of my Mom, I listened intently and eagerly.

Eddie walked down the hallway and passed by our conversation as he headed to the bathroom. He turns around and pops his head into my room.

"There really is something Oedipal about this, you know?" he says derisively. Mom says nothing in response. And yes, while I was in high school, I knew of Sophocles' play *Oedipus Rex* and what it is about. I took great offense.

Did I voice my offense? What do you think?

Shortly after Ed passed away in 2002, I lost my job at that radio station in Eufaula. And I had to move back in with Mom and Dad for a while as I got back on my feet. Sadly, temporary became way more permanent than I would have liked.

As I lived with them again, I saw Mom's rapid descent into her deep, dark hole.

Mom would rarely sleep. She stayed on an old beat-up fold-away sofa in the guest bedroom. Which ironically was Melborn and Martha's master bedroom once upon a time. She rarely slept in the bed with Dad.

Her self-medication was out of control. Bad food, near round-the-clock drinking, and mindless TV were her only friends.

Mom's body held on for a few years after Ed died. But her spirit was gone. Absolutely gone.

To her credit, she managed to get back into therapy. But I had a hunch that she wasn't taking it seriously. She had manipulated her therapist so deeply that they did very little work. Talking about dogs and not talking about what was going on in her head.

Hell, Mom even admitted this one time! She was proud that she was able to have a conversation with her therapist about such trivial things. And to be fair, these were important things to her, but it didn't do a thing to help her heal.

And while I was in my 20s as I saw all this, I was emotionally immature. I couldn't see the truth of what was going on right in front of my nose. And the truth was that Mom wanted to die. While she didn't take the big, dramatic act of ending her life, she essentially committed suicide on an installment plan. Over many years. Accumulating tons of interest that I'm still paying off many years later.

I was completely blind and willfully ignorant to the truth of what was going on with her. I just figured she was being a pain in the ass.

I wish I was right. Oh do I wish I was right.

One night I went to use the restroom and I saw Mom walking down the hallway. She acknowledged me, but I could tell she was gone. I noticed two things about her that terrified me. I noticed she had what looked to be scratch marks on her wrist. They didn't appear to be deep cuts, but simply scratch marks. And I also noticed just how yellow and jaundiced her skin and eyes appeared to me.

This was the moment I realized just how sick my Mom was becoming.

I have always and will always say that Mom is the most intellectually intelligent human being I've ever known. I believe if she'd kept taking care of herself, and had kept the confidence I saw as a younger child, I truly believe she'd have gotten her Ph.D. and become a college professor somewhere. She might've even gotten into college administration.

**

Even when she was younger, Mom was never one who enjoyed entertaining people. But as she got older and deeper into her mental illness, she actively avoided it.

However, in August of 2003, she got it in her head that she wanted to throw a party for Dad on his birthday. Never in my life had I remembered her choosing to do something so...out of character.

Don't get me wrong, Dad was an active enabler in this behavior. He rented a pressure washer and we pressure washed the driveway. I remember burning my arm helping him to lift it into the back of his truck after we were done pressure washing the driveway.

For the party, they got - I can't believe I'm about to write this sentence - they got a keg! My parents were in their 50s at this time, yet they saw fit to get a keg.

The day of the party was so unbelievably bizarre. I found myself feeling obscene levels of anxiety about this whole experience. I didn't know who was going to be there. Other than this one guy named Marcus who lived in a trailer that he plugged in at one of my Grandfather's old barns, I didn't know who was going to be there.

Yeah...at my Mom's urging, she allowed this guy Marcus to plug his trailer into the power in one of Granddaddy's old barns. She'd let him do laundry inside our house! This was a man who could've been a serial killer.

I was first introduced to him as he was playing a criminally out of tune guitar for Mom and Dad one night when I came home. I made a joke about feeling like I walked into the middle of an episode of *Austin City Limits*.

"I was once on that show." Riiiiiight...and I've got a hot date with Scarlett Johannson at her palatial oceanfront estate in Scottsdale. I'll be flying to meet up with her on my pig.

Anyway, back to this asinine party. I came outside and I recognized a few people. There was a man wearing a Tony Stewart t-shirt with the sleeves cut off, jorts, and no shoes. It was the middle of August and I'm sure the driveway pavement was well north of 100 degrees.

I immediately feel a knot in my stomach. I didn't feel like I was in danger, but I certainly didn't feel safe.

Dad went around the room and introduced me to a few of the people there. Some I knew - like Marcus and his atrocious-sounding guitar. But when we got to the man manning the grill, he introduced himself as:

"Call me Bugs, man." I took a beat to absorb that news. Did I hear that right?

"I'm sorry, did you say Bugs?" I had to get confirmation.

"Yeah man, like Bugs Bunny." I heard it right. This was a grown man who called himself Bugs. Was he an exterminator and the real-life version of Dale Gribble from *King Of The Hill*? Or was this a Houston County, Alabama good ol' boy named Bugs?

At the time I desperately wanted a meteor to fall on my head, so I didn't ask for confirmation.

The party that afternoon ended up being an uncomfortably easy-going affair. I never felt comfortable, but I also saw how much Mom was drinking. And I was damn sure not comfortable with this.

Bugs cooked a mean burger, though.

The next morning I'm outside. I'm finding myself wondering why my 50-something parents would throw a kegger? This was Sunday morning and Mom had started going back to her old church. And since Mom hadn't driven in years, Dad drove her everywhere. And before they pulled out, Mom grabbed a plastic cup and poured herself what I'm sure was a pancake flat beer from the keg.

This was all normal in my eyes.

After going to therapy for a year or so, I think her therapist got sick of her manipulation and convinced her to go to rehab. I had no idea this was going to happen, but I got roped into doing this.

"Ryan, get ready. Ann wants to check into Bradford," Dad said to me. Bradford being Bradford Health Services outside Birmingham. This is a drug and alcohol rehabilitation facility.

"When does she want to go?" I was excited that she finally wanted to take this seriously.

"She wants to go tonight." I looked at the clock - it was already past 7 pm. The sun was setting quite late as we were in the middle of July. "And we want you to drive."

We didn't leave until after nine. I was already tired and scared, but I said that I'd drive. To be fair, Dad was also drunk as well, so neither one of them wanted to drive.

Let me paint the picture for you. We piled into my Dad's 1992 GMC Jimmy with more than 200 thousand miles. I drove. Dad sat shotgun. Mom sat in the backseat. This was looking to be about a seven-hour round trip. We got there after midnight and got home around 5 the next morning.

I was unemployed at the time, so I didn't exactly have to get up for work the next morning.

We dropped Mom off at this artificially quaint, faux rustic-looking building in the middle of nowhere, Jefferson County, Alabama. It's essentially what you'd imagine a drug and alcohol rehab facility in the middle of the country in Alabama would look like.

But I was convinced this would save her life.

Two weeks later, we had a family weekend. Essentially what family weekend ended up being was a 72-hour-long al-anon meeting. But this was before I even discovered 12-step for those who aren't in active addiction or recovery.

During one of the sessions during family weekend, the speaker said one of the most profound things I have ever heard. What this man said supported me in every coaching relationship I've ever had - as both a coach and client. It was the most profound explanation of gratitude and asking for help I have ever heard. The speaker was in recovery himself.

"I've gotten into the habit of taking my shoes off and sliding them under my bed just far enough for me to have to hit my knees to get them every morning and take them off every night. When I hit my knees in the morning, I simply say 'help.' I'm asking my higher power for help. When I take my shoes off at night and I hit my knees to put them up, I simply say 'thank you.'"

The plan was to have Mom stay at Bradford for a solid month - 28 days. But we had a surprise passenger in the car when we went home that Sunday.

To be fair, Mom kept up with going to meetings and aftercare after she left. This lasted only a few months.

After a few months, I came home one day only to find Mom with multiple empty beer cans in front of her. I was personally hurt as I looked at her so defeated, and neck-deep in her depression again.

"Really?" I asked incredulously.

"It wasn't working. I tried everything I could, but it wasn't working."

This led me to say one of the most judgemental things that have ever left my lips.

"I'm sorry to say but I'm disappointed in you." This hurt Mom and I'm regretful to this day that I said it. But I believe I needed to say what I said. I muted so much of myself, my personality, and my voice because I never wanted to make her upset. I never wanted to cause her any trouble. I changed who I really am to take care of her and protect her. And at that moment, I felt like I failed her.

I failed HER!

As I have said before, my Mom's spirit died when my Uncle Eddie died. Her body held on for a few more years, but her spirit was gone.

I was finally able to get out from under that roof in 2008. And it was because I partnered with Mom and Dad to build a house on our lake property in Ashford, Alabama. A house that I truly miss, but I don't know if it ever became a home.

It was only after gaining a little distance that I started to get present to how sick my Mom was. Because as I was under their roof, I was convinced that she was faking everything for attention. I did not believe that her illness was indeed an illness. I thought she was being a pain in the ass simply to be a pain in the ass. It wasn't so much that I couldn't see the truth, I think I chose not to acknowledge the truth.

For years when she'd go to the doctor, she'd complain that her doctors always told her that her liver enzymes were elevated. She'd take offense to this because, well, I don't think she wanted to know how sick she was.

Well, we all found out right before Thanksgiving 2008 when she was admitted to the hospital. She had started to carry tons of fluid that she couldn't get rid of. Essentially her liver had started failing.

But would she listen to the doctors? Would she stay with her treatment plan?

"I'm not staying! I will eat Thanksgiving Dinner at my son's house!" She talked her way into getting out of the hospital when she really should have stayed. Truthfully, she could have been put on the transplant list.

And no, I didn't make an entire Thanksgiving Dinner. I would have burned my house right to the ground. I got talked into grilling burgers for Thanksgiving Dinner. Because this is what my Mom wanted. She wanted to eat burgers at my place. And I obliged.

February 2, 2009

The Monday after the Super Bowl, I got a text message from Dad while I was at work.

"They just took Ann to the hospital in an ambulance. It's bad." I completely freaked out and left for the hospital immediately.

When I got to the ER and found her and Dad, Mom looked defeated. Her skin was yellow and jaundiced. Her eyes had no life or light.

"I'm glad you could come," Mom says to me with great difficulty. "You look really nice." I was wearing a lightweight blue sweater with khakis.

I didn't think I looked particularly good, but apparently, I did. And I completely blew off her compliment because I thought they were the ravings of a woman who had lost control of reality.

Ivy wasn't there yet. She was living and working in nearby Destin, Florida, and had hopped in a car as soon as she got word. She was about 90 minutes away. I was more like five minutes away.

I remember sitting in the ER with Dad after they took Mom away for some tests. We sat there in silence for several minutes, neither of us wanted to say anything.

Finally, I felt called to say something.

"What'd you think of Bruce's halftime performance last night?" Bruce Springsteen played halftime of that year's Super Bowl.

"I didn't watch it," Dad answered quickly. He looked at me with a look that could only say 'now's not the time.' Lord only knows what he saw before he called 911 the next day.

After she left the ER, she was admitted straight to the CCU. That was the longest week of my life.

A few days into her stay - I was not going to work - I walked outside with Dad. I took a seat next to him on a bench. He wanted to smoke a cigarette and I didn't need to be alone.

"Are you resting at all?" I ask him.

"Yeah, I am, surprisingly. I've been plying myself with vodka and pot. It's the only thing that's worked."

February 8, 2009

Around 3 in the morning, I get a call on my cell phone.

"It's time," was all that Dad said to me.

I put on some clothes and got in my car. And I knew this would be the final time I'd get to see my mother.

I watched Dad - with his hand shaking - sign the Do Not Resuscitate form as Mom had a living will. And we all got the chance to say our goodbyes.

As I stood at the foot of the bed, I felt anger and bile building up in my soul. I was about to say my last words to my Mom before she officially left her body, and I found myself feeling so much anger and rage.

"How could you do this to us?! How the fuck could you do this to us?!" I must've gone on for several minutes. I don't remember what I said because I was conscious for none of it.

After we all said our goodbyes, the nurses led us into a little anteroom to wait until the power had been cut to her life support, and she was officially gone. On the floor in this room was this white hazmat suit hood. And I managed to spend the next 20 minutes making Ivy and Dad roll with laughter as I talked trash about that hood. This was the best material I have ever had!

If only Ivy and Dad knew how badly I wanted to die at that very moment. I mean, I guess Ivy will once she reads this book.

5:42 AM...she left her body.

I had a dream a couple of years ago where Rachel Maddow interviewed Dr. Ann Ivey Hall, University Of Alabama President. This interview was concerning a story that took place at my Alma Mater.

In my dream, my vision of her was what I imagined a 71-year-old Ann Hall would look like. She had a solid white shock of tight, curly hair, and spoke with the confidence, intelligence, and passion that I know she always had.

But it wasn't meant to be.

Despite all her problems, I can't help but think back to that Monday afternoon in February of 2009. The final coherent thing my Mom ever said to me was a compliment about how nice I looked.

Mom's mental health by the end...let's be fair...it was fried. She was dangerously and deeply depressed and she loathed her very existence.

My Mom was the smartest person I have ever known or will ever know. Ann Hall had a beautiful mind. But she truly had a damaged soul which led the world to never truly know how brilliant and beautiful she was.

Despite the pain, the heartbreak, the depression, the alcohol, and the self-loathing, I'm comfortable in saying this; she really did love her people.

And she was so very proud of me.

Chapter 13

I can rarely think of a time when the Hall family didn't have a dog and a cat.

Mom and Dad adopted Cotton before I was born. She lived to 16 years old. Cotton was a jet black poodle mix named after the *Little Rascals* character.

She was a sweetheart of a dog who - to be fair - probably held on longer than she needed to. She was in very poor health when Mom and Dad had her euthanized.

We also had a cat named Buckwheat. She was an indoor/outdoor cat with black and white markings that were really beautiful. The thing I remember most about her was the fact that she'd sit by the door and yowl if she wanted to come inside. Likewise, she would yowl at the door if she wanted to go out.

I mean, she was a cat after all.

There was also this dog that Mom saw get put out by the side of the road. We were driving along and saw this happen right outside Webb, Alabama on our way back home. Mom flipped out, and we turned around and got her. She was a small schnauzer-looking dog.

It turns out she had heartworms. Every day Mom or Dad would give her a liver-colored pill that she'd take with great enjoyment. Beef flavored medication, y'know? Being all of seven years old, I grew to believe that the spots on this dog's belly were the liver pills we were giving her.

This little dog's name...Alfalfa.

Do you see the connection with all these names? How Mom and Dad became so enamored by *The Little Rascals* is a mystery I'll be surprised if I ever answer.

Side note: Ivy once had a Cabbage Patch Kid doll named Darla. She spilled soda on her during our flight to visit uncle Eddie in Miami and the stain made her look like she had a tan line.

Long story short, I've always had a kindred connection with animals. This makes me wonder why I didn't get a pet of my own until I was well into my 30s.

For the entirety of 2013, I started getting this nagging feeling that I wanted a pet. To be fair, I believed I needed something to help with my crippling loneliness. I think it was way more than that.

After the deep, dark depression of my 2012 and 2013, I was barely beginning to come out of my hole.

On a deep level, I felt like I wanted to have something to take care of so I'd be less likely to check out. If I had something to be responsible for, I might not kill myself.

Depression is an evil monster, y'all.

One day in late January 2014, I walked into the Wiregrass Humane Society outside Dothan, Alabama. This place is one of the most heartbreaking places imaginable. I mean no disrespect at all toward them and the beautiful people working there, but the shelter life for an animal is still a depressing existence.

I walked past several dogs that I felt a draw toward. Something about their energy just drew me in. But nothing clicked.

Maybe a week later, I went back. When I was there, I walked past this really sweet Shepherd-looking dog. We went on a short walk, but the connection wasn't quite there. I wonder what happened to that good girl.

Maybe one more time, I went back to the shelter and came back empty-handed. I was beginning to think this was going to be yet another way that I'd overthink myself out of happiness.

Patterns, man...

A couple of weeks later led us to February 17, 2014. I was walking the corridors of the humane society and nothing was jumping out at me. This was until I rounded a corner and saw this sweet, outgoing, and confident solid white ball of energy with a mysterious brown splotch on his right ear.

I bent down and put my hand inside the cage for him to sniff me. When he did that, I felt an energy course through my body. There was a deep connection already.

"I think I'd like to take this one for a walk," I say to the attendant.

"Be careful. This one's a handful," she says back. As soon as the attendant opened the gate to his cage, he did something remarkable. He went outside to this dog run area...and he peed! Y'all, he was already partially housebroken! "This is Pete. I'll let y'all get to know each other a little bit."

During our walk, he was rambunctious and a little uncontrollable. However I remember during our walk, almost instinctively yanking on his leash. He turns around and looks at me with his soulful, and human-like, brown eyes. Almost as if he was saying, "Yes, human?"

More than anything, there was a connection. This was a connection that felt real and powerful. And when we got back to the building, I said maybe the most important words I have ever said up until that point.

"I think I want to take him home with me."

The next morning I was sleeping at around 6:45. And I heard what I thought was a water faucet going off in my living room. When I came to and walked into the living room, I spotted my bundle of joy emptying his incredibly full bladder on my living room floor.

Notice I only said "partially" housebroken. Training would begin post-haste and forthwith.

A few months later in early May, I got a phone call that I was afraid was coming, but it still didn't lessen the blow.

At this time, I was working for a company called Premium Retail and my job was selling premium Samsung TVs at Best Buy in Dothan, Alabama. While my program was very successful throughout 2013 into 2014, Samsung chose to end its relationship with Premium. And I was also quite successful - I was the number one rep out of better than 200 in the program in back to back months in early 2014.

But, since my store was one of the smallest stores in the entire chain, I was near the top of the list to be let go.

This wasn't an easy phone call to receive. But I had seen the writing on the wall for several months. After I got off the phone, I found myself sitting in my recliner trying to absorb the news. I wasn't angry. I wasn't sad. I wasn't pissed.

Even though I saw the writing on the wall, I think I was in shock.

Pete watched this entire thing unfold. The hamster wheel in his head was spinning. He could tell I was spinning my wheels in the mud.

He started to tug on my pants leg and he began furiously wagging his tail.

"You need to go outside?" Answering my question, he grabs a ball from behind the sofa and trots over to the door. "Okay...I see you," I said.

I opened the door to the back yard and we had a glorious game of fetch. Only in his early going, Pete's idea of fetch was "run and get it but make human chase me." This made me laugh and I got back into my body a little bit.

"There may be something to this doggie human thing." I had absolutely no idea. Little did I know but that December, that good boy would save my life.

The absolute pinnacle of who Pete has become for me started at around 3:15 on the morning of December 23, 2014. This was around the time I got a phone call from the hospital where my Dad was staying.

"We don't think he's going to get any better. It's time to come down." So I called Ivy to let her know. We had some choices to make.

I walked into the living room and found Pete in his kennel. He looks up at me with the saddest expression that any creature has ever looked at me. He was also quite confused when I let him outside at 3:30 in the morning.

I remember as I pulled out of my driveway to head to the hospital, he poked his head out from behind the curtains to my front window to watch me pull away.

He knew.

When I got back home after making that fateful trip, he proceeded to stay by my side for a solid week. He stuck to me like velcro. He was there for every tear, every sleepless night, and every time I questioned if I wanted to go on.

His granite head became glued to my lap. He saved my life, I know he did.

The following summer, I was on a coaching call with my original coach. Other than dealing with estate drama, and barely allowing myself to grieve, my biggest project was completing my first book.

And oh my God, did I want to quit. Over and over and over, I wanted to quit.

There were two things that kept me grounded. The first was my coaching group and I will speak further about my coaching journey in a future chapter.

The other thing that kept me grounded was Pete. He kept me centered, laughing, and connected with my childlike self.

I mean, he probably shredded pounds and pounds of papers. He chewed up my DVD of *Deliverance* that I couldn't return to Netflix - which I never got a chance to watch! He got a green pen off of my desk and tracked green footprints on my floor. And he managed to get a green splotch on his chest that looked like he had a green heart.

Separation anxiety - I am not a fan.

Getting back to the day of my coaching call: July 2, 2015.

As soon as I clicked off the zoom call with Michelle, I saw a UPS delivery driver pull up and drop a package off at my front door. And Pete started to raise hell barking when he saw him.

I knew what this was. I knew exactly what this was. And my heart jumped up into my throat.

I open the front door and take the small package inside. With shaking hands, I cracked the packing envelope...and pulled out the proof copy of *Written In The Stone*. My book! My baby!

At this moment, I saw an almost 30-year dream come true. I was able to see the words that I bled, sweated, and cried over for almost three years. They were printed and bound in a paperback book.

I was officially an author!

As I saw the words I created unfolding on the pages before me, I couldn't hold it back much longer. I must've cried - I mean ugly cried - for two solid hours. This was it! Holy shit this was it!

I'm sitting on the living room floor cross-legged. There was something childlike about this moment.

For the life of him, he couldn't understand why I was so upset. Tears of joy weren't a concept to him.

He comes over to me and starts to gently lick my face. He then lays on the floor and puts his head on my lap.

He really is the goodest boy.

In closing, I think you might want to hear from the dog who saved my life.

I'm serious! You're about to meet him!

"Pete, c'mere!"

"What, human? I'm chewing my foot."

"I want you to meet the human who's reading this book." As I'm writing this, Pete looks at me and twists his head. "I'm serious. You can speak."

"WOOF!"

"Use your words, dude."

"Will they understand me?"

"I'll translate. I have two questions."

"Questions! I love questions!" Pete starts to twirl and wag his tail furiously.

"My first question is this. What made you choose me when you were in the shelter?"

"Hmm...the shelter?"

"The place you used to be in?"

"With the cows?"

"No, before that."

"OH! That place? You needed me. And honestly, I needed you. My first home wasn't all that good dog. They thought I got too big. But you always got me. You understood me."

"I did?"

"Yeah. When your face leaks, you know why I'm being nice, right?"

"Yeah."

"When you get really mad, when I start to shake, you get that. We get each other."

"I've never heard that put so eloquently. Thank you."

"And you said you had another question?"

"Yeah...why can't you call me Ryan?"

"I've told you, I have trouble with my R sounds."

"But you just said you did–" Pete sticks a paw in the air to silence me.

"You're my human. That's why I call you human."

"I'll accept that. We'll go out soon."

"Good, cuz I'm about to be a bad dog."

"Thank you. Thank you for everything for all these years."

"You're welcome, Ryan. That's why I'm here."

One final note here. I remember sharing a picture of Pete on the Wiregrass Humane Society Facebook page. And a commenter claiming to be Pete's original owner said something that gave me chills.

"He was named after Petey from *The Little Rascals*." Because of course he was.

He was destined to be my dog. He was destined to save my life.

Chapter 14

When someone you love dies, life eventually moves on. Life eventually goes back to normal. This is one of the unfortunate side effects of this process. While the mourners and grievers disperse, we're left to deal with the empty chair at the dinner table.

This is precisely what happened after Mom passed away. When she died, the mourners left. The "I'm so sorry for your losses" dried up. And life resumed again in its relentless pursuit of monotony.

This leads me back to one June 2009 morning at work at Vantage Sourcing - a call center where I worked for over five years. A day at Vantage was like *Groundhog Day*...over and over and over...only no Andie MacDowell was to be found.

One morning in early June I'm on one of my state-required 15-minute work breaks. Even in early June, it was already hotter than a firecracker. And all I wanted during this break was to sit outside at a picnic table by myself and not be bothered.

For context, this was less than four months after Mom passed away.

While I was sitting at the picnic table, I started messing around with my phone. This was before my first smartphone, so I had to figure out the framing without a front-facing camera. I managed to take what I'm pretty sure was my first ever selfie that morning. The horizon in the photo was slanted, but my face was there. And let me tell ya, there was very little life in my eyes. I looked shell-shocked.

Before I went back inside I noticed I had a voicemail from Dad.

"Hey Ryan, give me a call. I've got something I want to share with you." I waited until my lunch break to make the call. "I'll cut to the chase. Alan found out that Steely Dan is playing a concert at Orange Beach next Friday."

I know that Steely Dan - and particularly their co-founder Donald Fagen - were musical heroes to my Dad. Remember the record with the black cover and the silhouetted lady draped in the red ribbon?

"You need me to come over and watch the dogs for you?" I asked. Even though I was well into my 30s by this point, I still assumed the role of the dutiful child.

"No. I bought three tickets. You're coming." My stomach is fluttering at this point. I desperately wanted to come. The way he asked, it was if he needed me to come.

I stayed silent for a moment or two while I thought.

"Next Friday?"

"Yup," Dad says quickly.

"I don't think I have any PTO left." I used most of my allotment for the first half of the year when Mom got sick and eventually died.

"Well, you need to figure it out." There was an urgency in Dad's voice that I don't know if I was ready for.

I did figure it out. I switched around my schedule on that Friday and left early. And the three of us piled into Dad's truck and took off for Orange Beach. This would only be about a three-hour drive from Webb, Alabama so it didn't take a crazy long time to get there.

During the drive, only mere months after Mom passed away, there was a lightness and an ease about my Dad that I hadn't seen in years. Especially as Mom had been so sick in her later years.

We get to the amphitheater and park in their grass parking lot.

And Uncle Alan, being the master of tact and decorum, gets out of the truck, unzips his jeans, and starts peeing right in front of the truck.

A couple of Dan Fans walk by heading to the amphitheater while he's doing what he does. One of whom turns around.

"I'm just watering the grass." To his defense, he faced the truck as he relieved himself.

Yet still, what the fuck Alan?!

After we found our seats, Dad and Alan stopped by the concession stand for beer. I turned down the offer for a beer because I always felt awkward drinking around Dad. In reality, I think I wanted to fully experience what I was about to take in.

Except for Donald Fagen and Walter Becker, the band takes the stage. And they have a huge band. Their band has a four-piece horn section, a lead guitarist, three female backup singers, and the rhythm section - drums, bass, and keyboards.

I forget what they played, It was some sort of obscure jazz instrumental that I didn't know.

As they finished playing that, Walter and Donald came out to a huge ovation. I looked over at Dad and he looked like a little kid. He's so excited.

The drummer clicked off the tempo to *Time Out Of Mind* from their *Gaucho* album. And they played it with relentless precision and perfection. Ironically, this is a song about drug use...

I had no idea what would be in store over the next two hours.

**

Midway through the concert, they played the title track off that album with the black cover. If you're not familiar with the album version of *Aja*, it's a purposefully meandering eight-minute epic that can hardly be called rock, but Jazz-Classical. And it became iconic with tenor sax solos from jazz legend Wayne Shorter and radioactive drum breaks by Steve Gadd. And they play the song on stage exactly the way they play it on the album.

During the second drum solo - played by the remarkable Keith Carlock - I look over at Dad and he's got tears in his eyes. He's not exactly crying, but there's a wistfulness about him.

I draped my arm around his shoulder and yelled over the music, "Dad, are you okay?"

Dad smiles and says with a slight catch in his voice, "I can't believe I'm here."

Many years after Dad died, I shared this story with uncle Alan who had heard this story. This was his response to my story.

"*He was sad because he said 'I should be up there. I could still do this.'*"

Without even trying, this moment at the Orange Beach Amphitheater became the starting point of what ended up becoming a way that I could re-meet my father. A way that I could see my Dad for who he was at his core: my favorite music critic.

**

Now, when I was a kid, we'd attend several Atlanta Braves games almost every summer. And don't get me wrong, those were amazing trips. If I could have enjoyed those baseball trips as an adult I would have gotten tons more out of them.

Though I would like to share our "Pascual Perez gets lost on I-285" story.

Pascual Perez was a pitcher for several major league teams in the late 70s and 80s. He was signed by the Atlanta Braves and got called up to make a start against Montreal in 1982.

The Braves at the time were in a brutal slump - having won twice in their last 21 games. And even after that losing streak, they still managed to make the playoffs that year. It would be nine years until they did it again.

Pascual had just gotten his first-ever American driver's license, as he learned to drive in his native Dominican Republic. Even the most experienced drivers can get lost in the Atlanta freeway system, to say nothing of a guy who has never had an American license before.

I-285 is a city-wide bypass that essentially encircles the city. Instead of pitching in a Major League Baseball game that day, Pascual Perez kept missing his exits and probably drove several hundred miles. He never got to the stadium. He was hit with a $500 fine by the team for his trouble.

A few years after this, Dad and I went to a Braves weekend one summer. We had tickets to games on Saturday and Sunday.

We get to town on that Friday night. Dad managed to find a hotel near the Atlanta Airport and we ate dinner that night at a nearby Pizza Hut.

The game the next day was an early afternoon start. And yes, it was hotter than the business end of a rocket engine that afternoon.

We get in the car to head to the ballpark on the south side of town. And we got so dreadfully lost on I-285 that we barely made the first pitch. I think Dad eventually asked for directions at a Waffle House on the North side of town.

The year after that Steely Dan experience, I was online and I saw the lineup for the Seabreeze Jazz Festival in nearby Panama City, Florida. I attended the festival a couple of times by myself. I saw the late basketball star-turned smooth jazz maestro Wayman Tisdale play in back-to-back years.

The 2010 festival saw a big expansion. They moved from a small park to a much larger amphitheater and became able to attract much bigger names.

One of those names was Tower of Power. And yes, while they do NOT play jazz, they sure do play a ton of jazz festivals.

But they are NOT a jazz group! I refuse to let that drop!

From 1968 all the way up until today...

Of all the world-class music my Dad introduced me to, I introduced Tower to him. They came of age while my Dad was still playing music, but they weren't on his radar until I put them there.

The show was phenomenal. Mic Gillette, who was part of Tower's original lineup on lead trumpet and trombone, had come back for another go-around with the East Bay Kings of Soul. And it has often been said that Mic played the five most important notes ever played on a trumpet on a rock and roll song - TOP's first hit song *You're Still A Young Man*.

They played a deep cut that night called *Walkin' Up Hip Street* which is an instrumental from their *Urban Renewal* album.

At one point during this song, the only people left on stage were the rhythm section and Mic. Lead vocalist Larry Braggs and the rest of the horn section left the stage to let Mic have the spotlight. He proceeded to metaphorically light his trombone on fire for several minutes.

The entire show, I keep looking over at Dad. He's locked in tight and having such a good time.

I knew I had something.

**

The following summer I ran across something that gave me chills. Steely Dan was going to play the Tuscaloosa Amphitheater in its opening season in 2011. The date of the show would be August 20, 2011, the day after my Dad's 60th birthday.

We went up a day before the show and checked into the hotel.

This was also the first time that I'd been back to Tuscaloosa in about ten years. I needed to get reconnected with my roots.

When we got in, we had dinner at this sports grill near our hotel. And I think that restaurant has become the site of the radio shows for University of Alabama athletic coaches for better than 20 years by this point.

The next day we had all day to kill before the show. Dad wanted to stay inside the hotel room, but I needed to get out.

I borrowed Dad's truck and explored my old city. My first stop was my old house.

I pulled up in the cul de sac and got out of the truck. The new owner was outside doing some yard work. I wonder if he was the one who cut down that magnificent sycamore tree we planted right in front of the picture window.

"I used to live here. I just came to check out the old neighborhood," I said when he asked me what I was doing there.

"I don't give a shit." Boy, it sure as hell didn't feel like my home anymore. I had to get the hell out of there because I sure wasn't feeling much nostalgia. About the only thing that gave me any nostalgia was seeing my old basketball goal still standing. It was old and weathered, but it hadn't moved since I got it as a 10th birthday present.

I stopped by Northington Elementary School and the old army barrack building where I saw all those ink blots one summer Saturday morning.

The Tuscaloosa Amphitheater is stunning. It seats about 7,500 people and is situated right on the Black Warrior River. The sightlines were impeccable. The sound was immaculate. It was one of the most powerful musical experiences I have ever had. And it was something I wish like hell my hometown had when I was still living there.

When we got back to the truck after the concert, Dad looked over at me and smiled.

"Thank you."

We went on to see several shows at the "Amp" as the locals call it. We saw the Dukes Of September - a side project for Michael McDonald, Boz Scaggs, and Donald Fagen. And saw Earth, Wind, And Fire on an unforgettable Father's Day in 2013.

But the first time was the most magical.

As the years wore on, I noticed that Dad was getting slower and slower when we were walking back to his vehicle. He was getting winded a lot easier. He claimed his knees were bothering him.

To be fair, I would be in way better shape even if I didn't exercise. Dad with the smoking and whatnot...

Let's flash forward to early in 2014. I found out that Sir Paul McCartney would be playing in Atlanta. I picked up the phone and called Dad.

"To be in the same room with a Beatle - are you fucking kidding me? Let's go!" He gave me his credit card number and I bought two tickets.

The show was supposed to be in June. But due to some health issues, Paul had to postpone that show until October.

When the day of the show finally arrived, I had been chomping at the bit for months. I researched his band and what kind of setlist he would be playing. And even though he was well into his 70s, he was playing close to three-hour shows.

But I also noticed that Dad moved even slower. It used to drive me crazy that he'd walk so slow, but I always let him take the lead.

We caught a MARTA train from our hotel to the arena. I noticed that the train was about to leave and instinctively I started to run.

"Ryan! What the hell are you doing? We'll catch the next one." Oddly enough, this was advice I have taken to the New York City subway system. Something that New Yorkers will never understand.

The show was transcendent. It was magical. It was so beautiful. To be in the presence of the energy of one of the most important musicians to ever walk the face of God's green earth is something that mere language leaves me unable to explain. While he wasn't in great voice that night, his energy was through the roof.

At a McCartney show, one can expect a mixture of solo Paul and Beatles songs. And during *Yesterday* I caught a glance at Dad that in retrospect was more meaningful than I could have imagined.

The wistful look on his face belied how poor his health was at the time (and I didn't know the depths of the health problems he was suffering from.) And also, this was probably the first time we'd both heard *Yesterday* since it was played for Mom's funeral.

When we got back to the hotel room, we stayed up chatting until after 3 am. It was one of the best bonding experiences I ever had with him. I told him I'd been working with a coach and how much it meant for my first book. It was such a beautiful experience.

But when we finally turned in for bed, something took me all the way out. Dad pulled his shirt off to get in bed, and he had a lump the size of a bar of Dial soap on his belly. It really scared me, but did I say anything about it? Heck no!

**

On the afternoon of December 18, 2014, I got a call from Dad's friend Bruce that he just called 911. I was off work that day and I rushed over there. The last time I ever saw my Dad leave his house was in the back of an ambulance.

Around Thanksgiving that year we were hit with a cold snap. Dad had always been warm-natured. As he got older and sicker, he got way more cold-natured.

There was a space heater right in front of him that he had aimed directly toward his face. He was wearing socks and due to his diabetic neuropathy, he had next to no feeling in his feet.

He passed out drunk in his chair one night while the space heater was going on full blast. He suffered a burn on the bottom of one of his feet that he never properly got treated. I begged him to go see a doctor. He never did.

When he got to the ER, they ran some tests and they determined that he had developed a staph infection so severe (it was never just the burn) that they were going to have to amputate his foot.

I'm standing at the foot of his bed and the way he told me, it felt like he was a young child.

The first time that I heard about his cancer was when his doctor called to update us after his surgery. They found "spots on his lungs."

Dad had a full-body staph infection. And his body was too weak to fight.

He was admitted to the critical care unit – in what I'm pretty sure was the same room where Mom died – and held on for a few days.

Early on the morning of December 23, 2014, Tony Hall's spirit left his body.

And it wasn't until several years after he died that I was told that when he died that he had metastatic lung cancer. I'm sure that lump on his belly had something to do with his cancer.

If the infection didn't kill him, then cancer would have.

In the few days between Dad's passing and the funeral, I must've played *Long And Winding Road* from a McCartney live album on an endless loop. The first time it hit me, I was driving and headed to a movie. I had to pull over and cry for several minutes. It left me in a pool of tears if you know what I mean.

Let's just say, Christmas 2014 wasn't the most festive time of my life. And for the rest of my time, I'll have a grievance to air on Festivus.

2015 was a monumental year for me. It was maybe the longest year of my life up until that point. I mean, releasing a book, and traveling solo for the first time really made it special.

Aside from my vacations to Southern California and New York City, I made two solo concert trips that year, both to Atlanta.

The first was that May to see Rush. While I have never been a huge Rush fan, I felt called to take this trip. And I'm not regretful one bit. A spectacular show by a powerhouse of a band. I'm honored to say that I saw Rush play a show on their final tour.

That August, however...that was closure. Chastain Park Amphitheater in Atlanta - Elvis Costello opening for...yup, Steely Dan.

I had one ticket that I had to get on Stubhub. But I would be damned if I was going to miss that show.

I got to the facility and couldn't find a place to park to save my life. It was even an adventure getting to the parking lot. For reasons passing any logical understanding, they had two lanes of traffic headed into the amphitheater weaving through a residential neighborhood. That made about as much sense as...well...traffic lanes weaving through a subdivision headed to a 6,900 seat amphitheater.

When I finally found parking, I realized I didn't have the cash to pay for parking (I don't like carrying cash unless I can help it.) I found an ATM and went back to park. And I missed Costello's entire set.

No offense to Elvis, but that didn't mean a damn thing to me. I knew my assignment. I needed closure from the kids from Bard College.

I needed closure for Donald Fagen's biggest fan.

I found my seat. I was seated next to a family - a husband, wife, and two young kids. Usually, at an event like this, I like to make friends with the people sitting near me, but I didn't this time.

In two different realms, I needed this. Desperately, I needed this.

Just like every other time I've seen them play, the band comes out to play a jazz instrumental before they kick into their Dan music.

When the band took the stage, I had chills, and goosebumps, and I was about to sob in front of a family of strangers. But I didn't care one iota. I needed it.

The sound mixer that night had the drums mixed perfectly that night because I could feel every kick of Keith Carlock's bass drum. And it comes in strong on their opening song that night - *Black Cow* from their *Aja* album.

That entire show it was as if I could feel Dad's presence telling me "I've got you. You're safe."

There are still many days when I wish I could pick up the phone and call my Dad.

"What do you think of the new Tower of Power Album?"

"How about that Tide?"

"Does Derek Trucks compare as favorably with Duane Allman as his fans believe he does?"

"Our Braves - our beloved Atlanta Braves - just won the World Series!"

But more importantly than any of this, I truly believe I went from simply being a writer to an artist, the day that my Dad put that black album with the silhouetted lady in the red ribbon in my hands.

My Granddaddy and my Mom are how I became a writer.

My Dad is how I became an artist.

I quoted a Beatles song earlier that I played on an endless loop after Dad passed away. So long as I maintain a connection to the spirit world through music, I know I will never lose connection with my Dad.

That long and winding road will NEVER disappear.

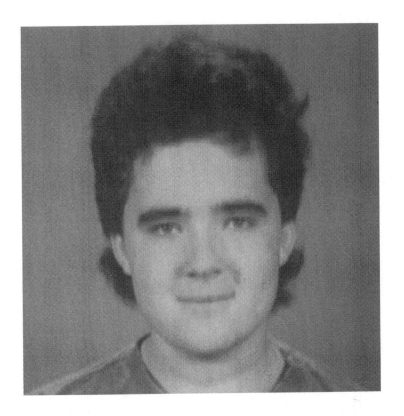

Sixth Grade School Picture Day

Ann And Tony's Kids - November 2017

Pete And His Human

Accomplishment Coaching - New York City
Winter - Class of 2017

My Yearly Christmas Eve tradition. I burn a
candle for love.

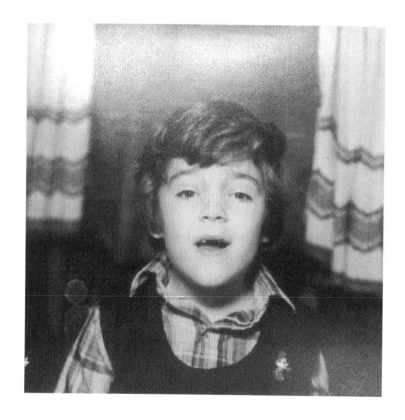

My Seventh Birthday

45th Birthday.

Chapter 15

Some of my favorite childhood memories were summer Saturday mornings. And as a kid, Saturday mornings meant one thing for me: cartoons! Thou shall not get in between me and my cartoons. Even if I'd seen an episode ten times, I'd watch anyway.

G.I. Joe, Inspector Gadget, Alvin And The Chipmunks, and Voltron were some of my favorites. I also had a weak spot for that Hulk Hogan cartoon, but I didn't want to admit it.

But my unquestioned favorite was without a doubt - Transformers. No irony at all that Big Ry has devoted himself to transformation.

Saturday mornings usually started with the Ann Hall Saturday breakfast special. Thick, fluffy pancakes, a couple of slices of Sizzlean bacon product (which in retrospect tasted a lot like what I imagine jerky dog treats would taste like), and an ice-cold glass of apple juice. Seriously, how 80s is that? All the while I'm watching Optimus Prime and the Autobots taking out the Decepticons.

My Mom had gotten involved with the 80s Tupperware party scene once upon a time. And so much of what we had in our kitchen was real, authentic, sho-nuff Tupperware. We had these dark green canisters on our kitchen counter where things like sugar, flour, and tea bags were kept. Our sweet iced tea was always served out of this one light brown Tupperware pitcher, which Mom would usually stir with this one dark yellow Tupperware spatula.

And we had these three Tupperware bowls. These bowls had flat bottoms and oftentimes she'd serve Ivy and me food in those bowls. And they came with little plates that cover the bowl, so they would have been good for meal prep.

Over the years, one of the bowls ended up falling into the bottom of the dishwasher and a part of it got melted by one of the heating elements. The way I saw it was that the heating element melted this tidy little slot for me to rest my fork when I was eating pancakes.

On other days when mom didn't make pancakes, we usually had cereal for breakfast. And we had these cereal bowls which were...guess what...Tupperware!

I mean, how 80s is this?

The holy grail of our Tupperware cereal bowls was this one white bowl. And let me tell you, Ivy and I had some of the worst fights ever about that dang bowl!

I seem to remember the white cereal bowl would end up meeting the same fate that the pancake bowl would. And oddly enough, I don't remember seeing it after it melted.

I can't help but wonder if it mysteriously ended up in the garbage as a way for Mom to get us to stop bickering about that damn bowl!

Many of the best memories that my family had growing up were at the Driftwood Inn in Mexico Beach, Florida. This was one of those super-charming little beachfront hotels that were run for decades by the same family.

In 2018 when Hurricane Michael wiped out so much of that part of the Florida Gulf Coast, one of the things that got taken out was the Driftwood Inn. And to say this broke my heart was a massive understatement. They have since rebuilt the hotel and have reopened it.

Let's get back to some of the better memories of that building. The hotel had two outparcel buildings apart from the main two-story building. And the Hall family usually stayed in unit 4B - which was one of those outparcel buildings.

We all loved this sleepy little beach town. Mom and Dad spent their honeymoon once upon a time at the Driftwood. And then many years later, they started to bring Ivy and me.

I remember one night we'd finished eating dinner. Dad liked to use one of the communal grills they had to cook chicken or burgers. After dinner that night, Mom and Dad had gone out to the balcony for some fresh air - and so Dad could smoke. And I was in the shower.

When I got out of the shower, Ivy was sitting in the middle of the communal living room watching this animal safari program on the Discovery Channel.

I sat down beside her and started watching. I believe this was inside a troop of monkeys or similar primates. The show we were watching had us deep inside the Amazon rainforest.

I looked at Ivy and said something funny about one of the monkeys. I might've said this in a silly voice that made her laugh.

Ivy picked up on this and started voicing over one of the other monkeys in a silly voice. We went on like this for the rest of the hour, absolutely cracking each other up!

We'd both continue these silly voiceovers when we started collecting Cabbage Patch Kids. Remember the cheese and the toothpicks and the spaceships?

And Ivy and I would make up these absurd voices for these dolls. We'd sit there in the back seat of the car and absolutely crack each other up. It used to drive Mom (who was usually driving) crazy, but we didn't care.

As younger mammals, Ivy and I were incredibly close. But as the family started to see more and more trauma, I started to isolate myself more and more. Because of this, Ivy and I started to grow further and farther apart.

I can't confirm this, but Ivy probably can after she reads this, but I get the feeling that she wanted a deeper relationship with me. But I was so scared of myself that I let it affect my relationships with everybody.

The older I got, I started to become deeply jealous of her. So much so, that some deep resentment started to grow and fester.

Think about it. I went through my childhood with a circle of trust that was closer to a dot. Primarily I didn't trust myself. And when you don't trust yourself, you can't let people into your circle of trust.

Ivy was two grades behind me. And for the life of me, I could never figure out why she was so much more popular than I was.

Granted, she was pretty, smart, outgoing, and had a magnetic personality. I always saw myself as having a magnetic personality, but with the magnetic poles reversed.

I have gone through much of my life with the feeling and idea that I'm playing with a

48-card deck. I have to work harder and move faster to get anywhere when many people get life handed to them on a silver platter.

And yes, I understand how ridiculous this is. I get it. But my inner 12-year-old is stubborn and you can't tell him a thing.

One of the resentments that started to grow and manifest as I got older and into my teenage years was the fear of talking on the phone. I mean, this says a lot for a guy who spent six years working at different call centers.

The phone rang at my house constantly. When you have a sister who's popular and you're, y'know, not - the phone was rarely for me.

After Mom and Dad moved back to Webb, Ivy and I stayed at the house for another couple of years. And when they moved out, Ivy was never at home. I mean, never at home.

Early on the morning of Sunday, March 7, 1999, the phone rings at 5 AM. This was one of those mornings that has become tattooed onto the back of my soul.

Over the years of Ivy being a teenager and having a ton of friends, I'd gotten used to the phone ringing at odd times. And usually, during this time, I could count on Ivy to answer the phone to deal with whatever teenager drama she was dealing with in her friends' circle.

For a little perspective, Ivy was 19 and I would turn 22 the following Friday.

So I let the call that morning roll to the answering machine. Not two minutes later, the phone rang again. This started pissing me off, but I let it roll to the machine again.

Barely one minute later it rings again. The hell with it, and I answered it.

"Ryan, this is Jennifer. I need to speak to Ivy. It's an emergency." Ivy had been friends with Jennifer for many years, but I didn't know her well. She had so many friends that it was hard to keep track sometimes. And to be honest, I didn't think much of Jennifer's admonition. I chalked it up to overly dramatic teenage girls being overly dramatic teenage girls. I woke Ivy up and she went into the kitchen to take the call. Why she didn't just take the call in her room I'll never know.

Not two minutes later I hear Ivy let out this blood-curdling scream. The pitch and timbre of that scream gave me cold chill flashbacks to the day Mom found out that Granddaddy had passed away while speaking on that very phone.

Oh, God...

"Joey's dead! Joey's dead!"

One of Ivy's best friends through grade school was this girl named Joey Barksdale. They were absolutely inseparable. She was a year younger than Ivy but managed to be in the same grade.

I don't remember much about Joey. She had sort of strawberry red hair and was quite soft-spoken at least around me. And had a very sneaky sense of humor.

A few hours before Jennifer's phone call, Joey and Ivy along with several of their friends were out on a Saturday night. Around 3 AM, Joey was driving along a rather perilous stretch of Hargrove Road in Tuscaloosa. This road has plenty of twists and turns. She lost control of her vehicle and ran headfirst into a tree. She was dead on arrival.

She was only 18 years young.

Ivy and I loaded into my truck and we headed to Jennifer's home in Northport. The sun was just beginning to peek over the horizon on this Sunday morning.

When we got to her place, Jennifer greeted Ivy and me with a tearful hug. Jennifer's father invited me inside but I politely declined. I didn't feel it was appropriate for me since I didn't know Joey as well as the girls did. And in retrospect, I wish like hell I took him up on that invitation.

As I headed home I turned the radio on. At the time I was working at a small AM radio station as the news and sports director. And our overnight programming was the rather unusual show hosted by Art Bell. They were talking about some sort of alien invasion in the desert in Nevada and I tuned out.

As I'm writing this chapter, I find myself getting present to something perhaps for the very first time. This might've been the very first time I ever saw Ivy as a human being. I always saw her as this ultimate social butterfly, able to make friends at the drop of a hat that neither of us wore.

Ivy and I both grew up in the same home. We both had the same beautifully damaged parents. But we handled life in a totally different way.

The older we both got and as deep as I got into my depression and my self-loathing, I felt like my understanding of who Ivy was being in her world totally dried up. It disappeared. We grew apart. It wasn't anything that either one of us did to the other, but we simply grew distant. We grew apart.

For many years, she was in a romantic relationship with a woman. Our family always accepted Ivy for who she was, but I personally never understood this relationship.

Keep this in mind, I'm seeing this from the outside. I never understood the attraction.

Her partner's name was Tina. And if I had limited understanding of who Ivy was being, I had less understanding of who Tina was being.

The time that Ivy and Tina were together was also during the time that I was living with my parents again. My vision of the relationship that Ivy had was tainted by Mom and Dad's rapid downfalls.

Every time I saw them together, I had a hard time understanding who they were being for each other. Their relationship felt cold and distant to me. And I heard reports of some pretty gnarly fights the two of them had.

They eventually grew apart and broke up. And Ivy moved down to Destin, Florida to eventually open a location of Panera Bread Company.

During this entire time, we simply weren't incredibly close. And I regret this. Especially as Mom's health started to take a severe right turn, I wish I'd been able to rely on Ivy for support as we both went through one of the heaviest times we'd ever go through. And I imagine Ivy would have wanted my support as well.

While she was living in Destin, she met and started dating a man named Billy. And if I had a hard time understanding who Tina was being, I had even less understanding of who Billy was being. They got married and recently celebrated their 13th wedding anniversary.

On the outside, he's a large, burly man with tons of tattoos. He favors WWE wrestler Kevin Owens, if KO shaved his head. And I didn't trust him as far as I could throw him when I first met him.

Over the years, I can safely say that he's become one of my absolute favorite people. And I will be going into reasons why later in this chapter.

After Dad passed away, Ivy and I inherited the task of sifting through the mess that was Dad's estate. Which in reality, was closer to three estates. Dad's estate included Mom's estate and uncle Ed's combined in a trust.

That year I felt like a wedge was driven between Ivy and me. And this isn't because we fought over the estate money.

I took on a lot of the lead work in getting the estate settled. Having meetings with lawyers, writing checks, and generally doing a lot of the leg work for settling the estate.

Ivy was still living in Defuniak Springs, Florida, some 90 minutes by car from the estate itself. And from my eyes, it seems like she got a little distant in her grief. And I understand why.

I can't speak for her, but I was quickly working myself into an early heart attack! And admittedly, a lot of my own grief got expressed in how I was handling the estate matters. I used the estate stuff to distract me from feeling my grief.

February 2019

I swear, what is it about the first week in February that has become so damn crucial in my life? Every single year. So many of the biggest moments of my life and my family's life have happened in the first week of February.

Ivy had been complaining about a sore throat for several months. And this sore throat wasn't getting any better.

She went to a doctor and the doctors saw something in her throat that greatly concerned them. And they ordered a biopsy.

As she's explaining this to me, I'm getting a terrible sinking feeling in my heart. Pain in her throat...biopsy...this is not happening!

And it should be noted that I'm living in New York, probably a thousand miles away! And I'm going through utter hell with my living situation there in suburban New York City. The less I speak about that in this book, the better. Perhaps in a future book.

The biopsy came back positive. My little sister had cancer and would begin treatment immediately.

And I was living a thousand miles away and there wasn't a damn thing I could do to help her. You want to experience the world's most helpless feeling? Because that's exactly what I felt.

She would begin a seven-week course of radiation and chemotherapy. Radiation five days a week and chemo once a week.

Ivy took a leave of absence from work as she fought this. And I wish I could have been there. What could I have done? Probably nothing, but at least I would have been there!

Her prognosis was always good. While it was stage III, it was always positive. It was always good.

But that word...after Dad, that word, man! That Godforsaken word, man. Cancer!

In all honesty, I was in one of the deepest mental health holes I have ever been in. I was about to get evicted. My mental health was dark, man. I had to talk myself off the ledge several times.

There was not much sleep to be had during these times.

I'd follow Ivy's treatment on Billy's Facebook and private updates. And I felt so removed from what was going on and it was driving me crazy.

From biopsies, to the procedure to insert her feeding tube, to radiation day after radiation day to chemo day. I'm trying to support my sister going through one of the worst times in her life while I was barely able to speak to her, it was killing my soul.

Iwant to give a massive shout out to Billy. He was there, every single day. He drove her to every single appointment. He worried himself sick. But he was there every single day. He never left her side!

Billy was an absolute rock star! He never left her side!

June 2020

2020, there's not a soul on planet earth who wasn't affected by the hell that was 2020. It was the darkest time...

The first half of 2020 for me...well, it was almost the end of me. I got let go from what I thought was my dream job. I got kicked out of where I was living right as the world started shutting down because of the Covid-19 pandemic and found myself living in a hotel.

However, one day that June I got a piece of news that I was praying and wished for.

Ivy's sore throat had come back. She had been complaining about it for a while even after the treatment was over.

Her doctors ran some tests and found that she had some irritation on the back of her throat. They were worried about the potential return of the tumor.

An immediate biopsy was ordered and a PET scan was also ordered.

And we waited.

The wait was interminable.

Until one day I was headed home from a grocery shopping trip on a city bus when I got a text message.

"It's negative!" Immediately I got off the bus and called her. I was still a couple of blocks from my stop, but I needed to call her.

"Is it true?" I asked.

"I'm cancer free!" Man, just writing those words again brings back the tears.

Growing up, I always saw Ivy as almost superhuman. She was able to get better grades than me. She was able to make friends easier than me. She seemingly was able to create her life out of whole cloth. While I...y'know...couldn't.

But since Dad passed away I have been able to see her as human. Imperfect, flawed, and fighting every day to make a life for herself and her marriage.

And the more I think about it, that's her superpower.

Chapter 16

Perhaps a 20-minute drive from my old Alabama home is somewhere that could have been my rock bottom. But instead, I believe it was where I found bedrock.

I was out riding in my car on the back country roads of rural Houston County, Alabama during the summer of 2012. I was in my car under the guise of building a business selling supplemental insurance for a dictatorial duck.

But I had a deep and unabiding fear of cold calling. I still do. I was never good at it and I couldn't stand doing it. And I tanked as an AFLAC agent.

"Hey, I'm Ryan. Wanna let me sell you something you don't need?"

Truth be told, I was at the end of my rope. I was done. I was as depressed as I've ever been in my life.

I was unemployed and had been for more than a year. By this point I was probably 50 pounds overweight even though I was going to the gym five days a week. I was simply ready to give up.

Near the Georgia state line, I saw this turn-off that I followed. This long and winding road probably snaked for over a mile until it ended at a small asphalt parking lot. What I found at this parking lot were a boat ramp, some picnic tables, and the Chattahoochee River.

It wasn't simply the water that I found fascinating. But this little park was right on a lock on the river. This is where water levels are raised and lowered for passing crafts - usually tugboats and barges.

I would end many days sitting in the parking lot of this park, listening to a regional sports radio show hosted by Paul Finebaum. I grew to hate this show but listened anyway. The entire time I would listen, I would wonder where it all went wrong. Where my life went wrong.

The winding road that leads to the water is surrounded on both sides by a treeline. And I remember one day when I was headed to the parking lot, I noticed something darting in and out of the trees up ahead. I got closer, and it was two young deer playing!

They had no care or worry about passing cars. They were playing!

As the months ticked off, AFLAC showed me the door. I was grateful anyway. I had no interest in continuing to do that. This is the only job I have ever had that cost me money. But I kept going to the river pretty regularly.

This wasn't an everyday thing, but at least two or three days a week, I'd go. I'd watch the water. And wonder where it all went wrong.

One overcast December afternoon, I was perhaps at the end of my rope. I drove out there one more time.

As I watch the water, the lock turns on. And the water starts to rush through, causing a rip current that I found mesmerizing.

That afternoon felt a little different. That afternoon, I felt a major pull to take a swim. And considering my fitness level at the time, and the condition of the water, this probably would've been my final swim.

I don't believe I was truly suicidal at this time. I do know that my life was going nowhere fast.

I felt a calling just then. I can't explain what I felt, but this was a calling that I have never felt before. There was a yellow legal pad on the front seat of my car. I found a pen and I started writing. I don't believe that the muscles in my left wrist were powering this pen. Something higher - much higher - was powering that pen.

I wrote three things on this sheet of paper. And I wish like hell I knew what happened to this sheet of paper.

1.   Get into therapy.
2.   Find a job.

3.　　Check into this life coach you've heard about. (More on her later in this chapter.)

This was December of 2012. This ended up becoming the most important to-do list I have ever made.

By the following February, I'd found a therapist who I clicked with. I stayed with her for the next four years. The following June I got hired by a company to sell Samsung home theater gear inside Best Buy. While it wasn't full-time, it started moving me out of the hole I managed to get myself into.

Along the way in 2012, I had gotten onto the mailing list of this woman named Michelle Akin. She was the life coach I mentioned in the third bullet point on that yellow pad. Michelle's coaching is geared toward creativity. And as the world's most frustrated writer and author, I found her fascinating. I think I read her emails for about a year, but I never did reach out to her.

Did I really want to get out of my way? I guess I liked staring at blinking cursors and having no idea when or how I'd complete my manuscript.

That all changed in early February of 2014. Again, what is it about the first week in February that's so damn crucial in my life?

I was at work when I learned of the passing of one of my absolute favorite actors -

Philip Seymour Hoffman. Hoffman was the king of the everyman actor. And compound this with the fact that a suspected heroin overdose took him (and with my own family's history with substance abuse,) this really got me thinking.

Over coffee a few mornings later, I found myself revisiting one of Michelle's emails. And in it, she writes about how her husband was fighting some insecurities about the rising star of a former acting classmate and a friend of theirs named Ellie Kemper. Ellie went on to star in a Netflix series as well as become a commercial spokesperson for Buick.

While Justin (Michelle's husband) lost interest in acting, he was finding himself filled with conflicting emotions over Ellie's rising star. Essentially Michelle's piece was about sitting on stockpiles of talent.

Hoffman's death was due in no small part to him not being able to get out of his way despite his prodigious talent.

Sitting on stockpiles of talent...

I cracked open my computer and started composing a blog post about Michelle's piece. And I shared it on my Blogspot as well as my Tumblr. And I tagged Michelle on Tumblr in the hopes that she'd possibly read it, but not thinking in a million years that she would.

The next morning I woke up to this comment on my blog post - from Michelle! It read something like "it doesn't matter if it's me or not, find yourself an ICF-certified life coach now!" There was some urgency to her comment that threw me off.

I opened up a new email and stared at the blinking cursor for an hour before I finally started typing.

"Hi, Michelle..."

Over the next two weeks, we exchanged a few emails and scheduled a sample coaching session.

Our connection felt immediate and kindred. Talking to her felt like a no-nonsense friend willing to give you tough love with a sense of humor. And I felt like working with her could be a major benefit. I slept on it over the weekend and hired her that Monday.

To this day, I tease her about this. But I think the most human part of our connection was that she took the skype call for our sample session in the bathroom with her laptop resting on the closed toilet lid. And let me tell you, the acoustics in the bathroom of her old Brooklyn apartment were PHENOMENAL!

My initial results working in her coaching group were amazing. Within four months of working with her, my dead-end job (the job I did very well but felt no upward potential) had ended. This was due to no fault of my own, but it ended. Samsung simply didn't renew their contract. And somehow I had managed to lose ten pounds simply by prioritizing my well-being.

Oh...and I'd gone from having not written a word in my manuscript in months to a completed first draft of *Written In The Stone!* All in those few months.

Maybe this stuff works? Maybe this coaching works?

After my Dad passed away that December, Michelle and our group stayed with me and supported me as I got back on my feet. They provided a loving kick in the ass as I emerged from my hole.

They helped me celebrate the publication of *Written In The Stone* the following summer.

And they were there cheering for me as I said "I think I want to move to New York." Y'know...after visiting there only once.

Part of our group program was that we'd get one face-to-face call with Michelle a month. And during our call one month, Michelle said something to me that I will never forget.

"Have you ever thought about becoming a coach yourself?" I mean...no. I thought I was still too broken to ever help anyone else.

Michelle is one of the senior leaders of a program called Accomplishment Coaching. And she asked if I'd be interested in joining the program. We spoke about it for a little while longer before she told me. "I think you'd really dig it."

As was - and still is - my wont, I thought for a few days until I emailed her asking for more information. We set up an informational call, I thought about it for a solid month after we had that call.

I mean, it sounded like an amazing opportunity for me. A year devoted to personal growth. But it was not a small monetary investment.

The day that Michelle shared with us that she was expecting her first child, I was headed into town to pick up some lunch. I had a nagging feeling like something was calling my name. Something transformational...

After I got home, I pulled up Michelle's informational email to find the link to pay my deposit. And following a workout at the gym that afternoon, I'm headed home when she calls.

"Are you fucking kidding me? You really did it?!"

"I did. And I'm scared to death."

"Don't be. You're gonna love it and they're going to love you!"

Flashing forward to the following February. I landed in New York and immediately regretted it. It was COLD!

On the first day of the course, I found a conference room where the parties were gathered. While Michelle was there, she wasn't tied in with this program. She was associated with another one of AC's branches at the time.

After a round of hugs - and this was the huggingest group of mammals I have ever met - I met my classmates. The group of humans I'd spend a weekend a month with for the entire year and grow to love like family. While I'd love to single out everyone in this program, I'd like to single out a few special figures who I grew to know and love as a family over the course of the year.

Before the course even started, we went around on a video call and introduced ourselves. I was wearing an Alabama Crimson Tide polo shirt that afternoon on this call. I also mentioned that I'm from Alabama. A few moments after I made this introduction, I got a private message.

"I have to ask: Roll Tide or War Eagle?" That was Jason - one of the program mentor coaches. That moment helped me feel at home. Since I graduated, he and I have become dear friends. After I moved up to Yankeeville as I call it, Jason took me on a tour of some North New Jersey landmarks, several of which were where scenes from *The Sopranos* were shot. And no, we didn't go to the Bing.

The first real connection I had with a classmate was with Emily. Our connection always felt unlikely. Emily's one of those uber-spiritual women who I have always been confused by (and still am.) But we simply hit it off. It was an unlikely relationship that blossomed into a brief working relationship with a short-lived podcast we partnered on. Emily showed me that men can be empaths and not only the light and airy women I'd always associated with that term...y'know like she is. And she usually called me "Ry." Few people could get away with that, and she was one of them.

My connection with Alex was adversarial at first. I didn't trust him as far as I could throw him. I saw him as the pain in the ass uber-successful little brother who couldn't understand why I - the older brother - wasn't as successful as him. At first, I was jealous of his easy confidence. But as I got to see him more and more, I began to see the challenges he went through as he grew into himself. He's an ambitious guy who ran an unsuccessful campaign for the state house in his native Indiana. Alex is happily married with a young baby daughter. And he also exposed me to my very first Jewish wedding which was probably my "I'm not in Alabama moment #993" since I moved up here.

Speaking of unlikely relationships, Ian intimidated the everlovin' hell out of me when I first met him. Built like a linebacker, and with an accent from deep in da islands, mon - he's from the Cayman Islands and flew to New York every month - I couldn't get a bead on him to save my life. But as I got to see him more and more, I got to see a truly gentle giant who would give you the shirt off his back. He's helped me so much in so many ways, and I consider him my Caribbean brother from a different mother.

One of the things that I wasn't crazy about joining this coaching program was that I had to complete working with Michelle. I was terrified about that because I made so much progress working with her. And also, she was incredibly supportive after my Dad passed away. And I am slow to warm up to new people like that.

My new coach was Lisa. And I - to be fair - don't know if I gave her the fairest shot at first. I was so used to Michelle's loose and easy-going energy and Lisa felt a little more corporate. Granted, she didn't come from the improv comedy world like Michelle did. Lisa DID have a corporate background, by the way.

I'll never forget the first interaction I had with Lisa after I learned we'd be working together.

"Do I need to email you some stuff I've been working on with Michelle?"

"Nah. Let's start with a blank slate," Lisa says with a coy smile.

"Sounds good," I said.

"*Well shit*," was what I really meant.

Over the course of the year, I let my anger and frustration with myself get onto her in our sessions many times. I felt like she didn't understand me and was being obstinate. In reality, she was simply leading me to the answers to my own questions and I was the obstinate one. Y'know, she was doing exactly what a great life coach does.

No details here. This stuff is confidential and always will be.

I ended up working with her for almost two additional years after I graduated from AC.

Our relationship improved tremendously and she has become incredibly valuable to me. And asking her to write the foreword to this book was a no-brainer. Like any human relationship, there were still hiccups, but it got a lot better.

I will share one big thing she said to me. This was maybe a year after I graduated from Accomplishment Coaching.

I was being self-conscious about how slow and easy I was speaking during our call. I associated slow speaking with lower intelligence. Perhaps this was a bias toward my own Southern background. Even though I was being very hard on myself that day (and many days,) she encouraged me to keep speaking in this manner.

By the end of our call that morning, Lisa says this to me. And it's tattooed onto my soul.

"I have to say, I have never seen you show up as authentically as you have right here and right now in this call. When you're like this, your presence is like a warm and comfy fireplace and it's a privilege to be with." Damn...just typing her words makes me tear up a little bit.

I made massive strides while I worked with her. I finished my first draft of *Hello Again*. I started dating again. And I moved from the only home I ever knew out of pure possibility.

Y'know, among many other things.

Few people in my life have ever seen me as completely as Lisa Pachence, and for that, I'll be grateful until my dying day.

The most important moment for me during my program year didn't take place during a working session. It took place in the lobby after the session let out.

What I'm about to share was one of the most important moments of my entire personal transformation journey.

I grew to believe my teammates were all smarter than me. And for the most part, I kept my mouth shut during class. Seeing everyone with growing client practices, and I'm still with a goose egg. I think I kept my mouth shut for the first five or six months.

But there was one moment when I felt like I came out of my shell. It was very late in our program year as it was cold on that Sunday afternoon. We were headed back to the hotel conference room after lunch when Lisa caught up with me.

One of my classmates was working through something. Again, confidentiality is the name of the game so I can't go into details.

"If she brings it up, why don't you work with her?" Lisa casually says to me.

Sure enough, she brought it up.

I don't know what came over me, but I spoke right up. I had every eyeball in the room looking at me - which is intimidating in and of itself.

I held a mini-coaching session with her in that room. Jodi Larson (our senior leader and a woman who scared the shit out of me for the first half of the program) and my friend Jason were at the table to provide backup. But I didn't need it.

After we got done with our session and she had an action plan, my feedback from Jodi and Jason, and from the rest of the class was glowing. And I was floating for the rest of the day.

After the session let out, I was holding court with several of my classmates and I spotted Jodi on the other end of this room talking with Accomplishment Coaching CEO Christopher McAuliffe who was leading the program that started the previous August. Jodi catches a glance at me and excuses herself.

She practically ran over to me and gave me a big bear hug!

"What you did in there today, we have been waiting for that all year! I am so proud of you!" To know that I had the respect of a woman that Michelle calls 'the wizard' and who was one of the founding members of the International Coaching Federation, I can safely say was the most important moment in my entire personal transformation.

While I envisioned myself as a successful coach like my mentors (and many of my classmates) it hasn't happened yet. But my interest in coaching has shifted.

The people I have coached and supported to complete and publish their books, I have had the time of my life. This is the work I have dreamed of doing.

I'm helping brilliant storytellers create books! Most of them are first-time authors! I'm relying and calling upon my coaching training and practice to help them get through the inevitable roadblocks that happen as you're putting your soul onto paper.

And Michelle, if you're reading this, I did dig it. I'm digging this work every single day.

Chapter 17

"Where I'm going, I won't have these reminders of what I lost, what was taken away from me. And I hope you understand, I was a broken man in my own hometown - need to find my own peace." - *Goodbye Carolina* Marcus King Band.

Can I let y'all in on a little secret? Do you promise not to tell anyone else?

Lean in close...

Closer...

I won't bite...

Ready?

I am a lifelong pro wrestling fan.

TBS would air *Georgia Championship Wrestling* (later WCW *Saturday Night*) at 5:05 central time. And then the Braves would play (and usually lose) at 6:05. It was like clockwork, I'd listen to Jim Ross, Tony Schiavone, and Bob Caudle call Dusty Rhodes, Ric Flair, and the IV Horsemen then I'd listen to Skip Caray, Ernie Johnson, and Pete Van Wieren talk about Dale Murphy and Bob Horner at 6:05.

For many years, that was my summer Saturday. I spent a lot of time alone, y'know?

During the Monday Night Wars between the WWF and WCW in the late 90s, one of my favorite wrestlers during this time was a man called Diamond Dallas Page. I always found him relatable and real. He was never one to sport the giant bodybuilder physique that prime Hulk Hogan, Lex Lugar, and the Ultimate Warrior (among many) carried. DDP was a guy who you could see having a beer and smoking a cigar with after the matches.

Another thing I found out about DDP was that he didn't start wrestling full-time until he was 35 years old. At an age when most star wrestlers have been practicing their crafts for 10-15 years, DDP was just getting started.

Diamond Dallas Page won his first-ever world championship in 1999 by defeating a member of the Mt. Rushmore of 80s and 90s pro wrestling - and my favorite pro wrestler of all time - "The Nature Boy" Ric Flair. Also in the match were Hulk Hogan, Sting, and "Macho Man" Randy Savage was the guest referee.

This was a veritable who's who in pro wrestling over the past 40 years.

After he stopped wrestling full-time in the early 2010s, he became a motivational speaker, author, and the world's most unlikely yoga guru.

I know, I know. "It ain't your mama's yoga."

He also became known for reaching out and supporting a few of his mentors and some of the men he traveled with who may have fallen on hard times. DDP supported them by helping them beat their addictions and helping them to deal with the numerous health problems that accumulate through thousands of body slams.

Page put up a youtube video in 2012 that was one of the most important things I have ever seen online. It truly changed my life. Discovering that it's been taken down broke my heart because that video meant a lot to me during a dark time in my life.

The "American Dream" Dusty Rhodes (speaking of a wrestler you'd want to have a beer with) was a mentor to DDP as he was coming up. He took him under his wing and helped him during his training and his salad days on the road.

Dusty was working on the booking committee with World Championship Wrestling in the mid-90s when DDP was first starting to make a name for himself as a wrestler. Page was no stranger to the wrestling business as he was a longtime wrestling manager before he started wrestling.

Page was at home and feeling some mounting frustrations. He picked up the phone and called Dusty. He had grown frustrated with his place on the card.

"I wanna go out there and steal the show. I know I'm getting better. But I know I'm never gonna be the main event guy. I just want to be at the bottom of the top of the ladder. I know I'm never gonna win the title." Page figured he started wrestling too late to get that main event slot alongside guys like Ric Flair, Randy Savage, and Hulk Hogan who all had 30+ year careers..

Dusty let DDP vent for several minutes before he cut him off.

"Are you through, kid? Cuz I've got a few things to say to you," Dusty says in his unmistakable Texas lisp.

In an act of tough love, Dusty proceeds to read DDP the riot act for the next hour. Essentially saying "if you don't believe you'll ever get there, then you damn sure won't get there."

After DDP hangs up the phone, knowing that Dusty was a straight shooter, DDP picks up a notepad and a pen. And he wrote, "Within five years I will be world champion."

A little over four years after that phone call, we're in Tacoma, Washington at WCW's *Spring Stampede* show in 1999. After DDP pinned Ric Flair in that four-way match and won the title, he was in the dressing room taking his gear off and about to get in the shower when he heard a knock on the door. It was Dusty. He pulls DDP into a congratulatory hug.

"How's it feel, kid?" Dusty asked.

"It feels real, Dream."

"That's cuz it is."

The youtube video where DDP speaks of this event in his life gave me an idea.

In October of 2012, I was about at the end of my rope. Dare I say, the end of the rope was around my neck just waiting for anything to pull it tight.

On that Thursday night in October 2012, I pulled out my computer and started writing. I wrote a blog post that ended up being the second most important blog post I have ever written.

The lesson of that youtube video was this simple phrase that DDP kept repeating.

"Don't just think it, ink it." Write down your goals to give them life.

I knew that my future wasn't in selling AFLAC insurance or anything else. I knew my real legacy was inside of my stories, my books, my plays, and my words.

In this blog post, I wrote this paragraph.

"Today is Thursday, October 18, 2012. I'm stating that within five years I will be in the

**creative business. I will be a produced playwright.
I will be a writer for TV or movies."**

It didn't work out exactly the way I
envisioned it. I'm still not a produced playwright
or working in TV or movies, but I am a
three-time published author. And it didn't take
me five years either.

As the years ticked off as I approached this
declaration, I kept getting this nagging feeling
that kept chewing at me. That feeling was that I
couldn't accomplish what I wanted to accomplish
while living in Southeast Alabama.

I needed to get out. I needed to truly
spread my wings and fly. And I could never soar
while in Southeast Alabama.

Oh sure, I could write from anywhere. I
wrote most of *Written In The Stone* sitting next
to Glen Lawrence Lake while sitting on my back
porch. But to truly get into the business I wanted
to get into, I needed to get out.

Leaving Alabama felt daunting. Dad wasn't
getting any younger, and I felt I needed to be
there for him as he got sick. He got so sick and
died so fast that I didn't have that opportunity.

**

After Dad passed away in December of
2014, I needed to take a few days' vacation. In

May of 2015, I hopped on a plane and headed to Southern California. I needed to experience it.

This trip was fraught with...stuff.

I made the mistake of booking a hotel in Redondo Beach, which I always assumed was in the LA area. I mean, I guess it is. But it's in the suburbs and 25 miles from anything.

Gorgeous, don't get me wrong, but not where I wanted to be.

And to complicate matters, you know...a lot, I managed to lose my driver's license at the Atlanta airport. Why the hell I didn't simply put it in my wallet, I'll never know. So the rental car reservation I made was out of the question, to say nothing of having to jump through serious hoops to get on the plane back home at the end of my trip.

I had an amazing time in California. I got to see Hollywood. I got a Roll Tide on Sunset Boulevard. I got to see my old and dear friend DeAngelo for the first time in better than 20 years.

One of the stranger highlights of my trip was during a bus tour I took of Beverly Hills. While on that tour, I saw that Gary Busey had a giant picture of himself plastered on one of his doors.

My friend DeAngelo took me to this rooftop bar in Santa Monica. It was in the middle

266

of the afternoon and many of the tourists were already well-lubricated. We met a couple of girls from the University Of Texas and one of whom - she was quite tipsy - stuck her hand in my face and invited me to smell it.

I'll leave it at that.

But it was in a quiet moment when I got present to how much freedom I was feeling.

I went to SoCal on the rare cool week in mid-spring. I'm sitting on this cool beach - alone. My toes are in the sand and I just felt peaceful. After the hell of the previous few months, I felt free. I felt light. I felt...alive.

When I got home I kept having this nagging feeling chewing at me. This seems to happen a lot in this portion of our story.

I needed to check out New York. And I needed to commemorate Dad's birthday in New York. August 2015 would be my Dad's first birthday in Heaven.

I stayed in this uber-charming little boutique hotel in the Greenpoint neighborhood in Brooklyn. My only real complaint was this hotel was right beside a Brooklyn school bus depot and school was just starting back.

That first morning, I found this charming little diner near my hotel called "Egg" which featured southern-style breakfast fare. While it was no Cracker Barrel, it was damn sure good. Granted, the pancakes I had were as big as hubcaps, but they were amazing! And my server was an exotic beauty who looked like she could've been Kerry Washington's little sister.

After breakfast, I started to explore the area when my coach Michelle texted me.

"I'd love to treat you to dinner. Meet me at this address..." This would be the first time I'd ever get to meet her in person. We had an amazing time and one of the finest meals I have ever had. Her friend was the owner and chef of this restaurant in SoHo (which has sadly closed down.) They featured gourmet comfort food that was to die for. The highlight of that meal was these cheeseburger spring rolls that...I could have made an entire meal off those damn things.

The next night I learned that Jim Ross, the iconic pro wrestling commentator from WWE and WCW, would be hosting a one-man show at the Gramercy Theater in Manhattan. I wasn't going to miss that!

He gets on stage and starts to riff for two solid hours without any notes. He shared stories that would make your hair curl about some of the guys he worked with. There was a story about Andre The Giant that involved a hotel clerk and a camera...and well...it's more than slightly NSFW.

"I just gots to know."

But I think the next day was when it hit me. The next day I'm sitting in this charming Brooklyn pizza shop having my first ever slice of real New York pizza. I'm surrounded by accents I have never heard before, languages you don't hear in Alabama, and more culture than you get in a year back home.

I had this thought come over me. This feeling was crazy powerful. And I will never forget it.

"Ryan, you're free. You're free."

After I finished my pizza, I went outside and couldn't help but start to sob. Not only was this the first time I'd been around so much culture and freedom, but the emotional independence and freedom were so liberating for me.

I needed the distance to properly mourn the deaths of my Mom and Dad.

When I got back to my hotel, I knew I was going to have the coaching call of all coaching calls that Monday morning. My group was about to get one helluva surprise.

**

"I think I want to move up here."

Without thinking or hesitating, I spoke those words. I said it. And now I had to live up to it.

Hell, I even went back to New York at the beginning of November to "look for a place to live." Yeah, that didn't happen. I got overwhelmed way too easily. I mean, why would anyone want to rent to me with my giant dog?

All during my Accomplishment Coaching year, my classmates kept pestering me "when are you moving to New York?" I even got into a pretty significant row with Lisa about why I hadn't made more progress in this.

But during this entire year, I kept thinking back to that original blog post. "Within five years..."

I made a further declaration that I would be moved by the time I turned 40.

I made the gut-wrenching decision to sell my beloved lake house. I loaded up a U-Haul, and Pete and I made the long drive. We stayed with my uncle Alan in Montgomery for a couple of nights. I'm behind the wheel of that U-Haul and for the two hours I'm headed to Montgomery, I'm sobbing my eyes out the entire time.

I really did love that house.

After a couple of days with Alan, we started the journey on March 10, 2017.

I got to the Charlotte area on night one.

I spent the final night of my 30s in Midlothian, VA on night two. I had dinner at a Hooters.

The next morning I woke up and we set forth for our target in Secaucus, New Jersey.

I'd been driving probably close to seven hours. I'm exhausted and hungry. And Pete is bored to tears and really needed to be a good boy.

I'm on the Jersey Turnpike and getting raked over the coals with tolls. Remind me never to drive a U-Haul on the Jersey Turnpike again.

But it was all worth it around 10:30 that night. Unfolding over the horizon was a glorious sight. It was the Manhattan Skyline!

"PETE! We made it! We're here, dude!" Granted, I am just crying my eyes out but all Pete needed was a walk.

But we did it! We're here! And on my 40th birthday!

We settled in Port Chester, New York. And have gone on to live in Stamford, Connecticut.

In the five years I've been up here, I have accomplished so much. This is the second book I've released - my third overall. I have a relationship with the iconic Capitol Theater in Port Chester where I'm one of their roster of concert reviewers. I am a graduate of both the

Landmark Forum and Advanced Course. I read from *Hello Again* at this uber charming little club in the East Village of New York City. And I am a graduate of the Writer's Hotel Conference and gained lifelong brothers in language along the way.

Even in the depths of my depression and hopelessness, I was able to gain a truly beautiful perspective on life just by writing down my goals.
I thought about it.
And I inked it.
And I'm barely getting started.

Chapter 18

In closing, I want to talk about a musical instrument. This musical instrument is one of the main reasons for so much of my personal transformation. To be clear, this is not because I love to play it. I can't play...

Donald Fagen, Stevie Wonder, George Duke, Larry Dunn, and countless other genius musicians specialized in this instrument. This instrument was a fixture in 70s soul, jazz, and rock music. The sound it would make could be a percussive walk or it can be a colorful melodic painting.

The Fender Rhodes piano is an electric piano that became wildly popular due in no small part to Billy Preston's use of it during the iconic rooftop concert that the Beatles performed in 1969.

That keyboard break during the bridge of the Beatles' *Get Back*? That was Billy lighting a Rhodes piano on fire.

Even though he hadn't played music professionally in more than 35 years, Dad never lost that desire to play. And his dream instrument was always a Rhodes.

I'll never forget this one call I got from my Dad in the summer of 2010. When I answered the phone, my Dad was practically childlike with giddiness. My Dad had been in a pretty deep depression since Mom passed away, and I absolutely understood why.

"I found it! I found one!" Dad says.

"Found what, Dad?"

An old friend of his from high school named Jimbo was selling off some of his musical gear and he called Dad and asked him if he'd like to take his Rhodes off his hands. Dad was all too eager to make the two-hour drive from his house outside Webb, Alabama to Montgomery.

With $500 cash in hand, he picked up this piano, a stand, and a small amplifier and practically floated home the next day.

The next weekend, Dad invited me over for lunch that Saturday. He enjoyed manning the grill and frankly, I enjoyed eating what he made. I always enjoyed our bonding time after Mom passed away.

Dad was lonely. He really didn't have much family left after Mom died; just me and Ivy. Ivy lived two hours away, I lived five minutes away.

That Saturday when I arrived at his house, I saw the piano set up in his mudroom. The key cover was off and she was plugged into that amp.

274

"Hey, Dad? Let me hear something. Let me hear a little *Home At Last.*" I secretly knew he would be shy to play anything. He spoke about getting his chops back like it was some sort of mythical creature and I figured he'd use that circumstance to keep from playing something for me. Especially something played by his hero - Donald Fagen.

I think he pretended not to hear me and I chose not to push it. Even well into my 30s by this point, I still felt like a little boy at times.

A few months later, I was over at his place and he said something that lit my soul up.

"I was talking with these guys the other day and they wanted me to sit in with them." When I say that lit up my soul, I'm talkin' Times Square here!

I was so damn excited! I just knew that his depression could be helped so much by getting reconnected with music.

"I just need to get my chops back." That's musician-speak for needing to get good at his instrument again.

Dad never did get his chops back.

As the years ticked off, Dad got deeper and deeper into his depression. He was smoking more and more marijuana as well as those Black and Mild cigars. He was drinking heavier. He was letting his despair get to him. And his physical health was getting worse and worse as he spent some time in the hospital.

And the dust on that piano started piling higher and higher.

I remember coming over to his house shortly after he passed away and was horrified to notice that the white keys on that piano had started turning gray from the amount of dust built up.

I believe at this moment I made an unconscious choice to uncover my own voice. I couldn't articulate it at the time, but I believe that was the moment.

I couldn't abide another dusty piano in my life.

I found a Swiffer dusting cloth and cleaned off the dust. I turned on the amplifier and plugged the cable into the piano. While I can't play piano, I know what a Rhodes piano should sound like.

I plinked out a few notes and thought, "well damn. It sounds just like Fagen's piano."

Flashing forward a few years to my Accomplishment Coaching graduation dinner in January of 2017. I knew I was going to get called up to speak - we all did. Everybody there had someone in their life they would speak about there as their guest.

My body was by myself, but I wasn't alone.

When my name was called, a flock of butterflies started to move around in my stomach. I broke out in a flop sweat. I desperately tried not to cry. I failed.

I take a deep, cleansing breath...

"So hi..."

One of the most fun experiences of my life was the six-week improv acting class I took at this place in White Plains, New York. I was the only man in the class and I had a blast.

During this class, we played a game called Scene From A Hat. We got the script of a scene from *Charlie And The Chocolate Factory* and we were assigned a part to read. We drew slips of paper from a hat and written on this slip of paper was an animal name. And we had to read our lines in the character of this animal.

I was a snake. I was wallowing on the ground, slithering, and giving one of my classmates a legit jump scare when I hissed at her.

This was the most fun I'd had since I was a kid!

Earlier that year I was a participant in a class with Landmark Worldwide. Landmark is one of the leading personal transformation programs in the world.

Every Thursday night I'd hop on a Metro-North train into the City and I'd go to this building right across from Madison Square Garden. And these were huge seminar classes - several hundred people would gather at a pop.

As part of this seminar, the leader would invite people to step to the front of the room to share something in their life they needed support with - relevant to the context of the seminar.

I was always scared to do this because, well, that's a lot of people I could embarrass myself in front of. But I got a wild hair one night late in the 10-session seminar. And I stepped up. I spoke powerfully, eloquently, and with honor.

I stood at that microphone and looked out over the sea of faces. I felt no nerves, only purpose.

Back inside that quaint Italian restaurant in NYC's financial district at the graduation dinner...

I'm standing in front of that group of people and I'm trembling. I shove my hands inside my pockets to avoid showing how badly they were shaking. But little did anyone else in that room know but my colon was trembling, I was so nervous.

I open my mouth and start to speak.

"The person I want to speak about tonight isn't here in person, but I know he's watching and listening. So I'd like to tell y'all a story. Have y'all ever heard of a Fender Rhodes Piano...?"

So many of us have put our real and authentic voices in mothballs. And I pray that my story has helped you discover even a smidgen of the world-rattling voice that lay dormant within you.

It's there.

Invite it over for a playdate.

Have fun with it.

It's time...

It's time to shake up humanity with your voice.

So get to mining.

About The Author

RYAN D. HALL is the bestselling author of *Written In The Stone* and *Hello Again, and* he's a contributing author for two Amazon bestselling anthologies. Ryan is also the creator and host of the Soul-R Powered Podcast (available wherever podcasts are found. He's a writing coach and publisher, and he and his writing partner (his dog) Pete live in Connecticut. Follow Ryan: **twitter.com/ryanhallwrites.**

More From The Author

- *Royal Hearts Media* - Ryan's coaching and publishing services.
- *Written In the Stone* - Follow the story of journalist Ethan Whitehead as he uncovers a story that can shake the very foundation of the United States Government, all while he keeps his family from falling apart.
- *Hello Again* - "HERE'S MIKEY!" Follow Mike Holliday from the stages of his late-night talk show to his family's stage. *Hello Again* is a heart-warming novel about redemption, fathers and sons, and taking your genius out for a drive one last time.
- *The Great Pause - Blessings & Wisdom from Covid-19* - Ryan and 24 other authors share stories of resilience and triumph learned from their experience during the Covid-19 pandemic and shutdown.
- *Redefining Masculinity - Visions For A New Way Of Being* - Ryan and seven other authors share vulnerable stories about what it means to be a man in today's world.
- *Soul-R Powered Podcast* - On the Soul-R Powered Podcast, Ryan features stories of people who have used their resilience and transformation to live a more soul-centered, soul-r powered life. Available wherever podcasts are found.

Made in the USA
Middletown, DE
25 November 2022

15707465R00157